THE PERSONAL SPIRITUAL LIFE

THE
PERSONAL
SPIRITUAL
LIFE

Peter Masters

THE WAKEMAN TRUST, LONDON

THE PERSONAL SPIRITUAL LIFE
© Peter Masters, 2013

THE WAKEMAN TRUST
(Wakeman Trust is a UK Registered Charity)

UK Registered Office
38 Walcot Square
London SE11 4TZ

USA Office
300 Artino Drive
Oberlin, OH 44074-1263
Website: www.wakemantrust.org

ISBN 978 1 908919 20 5

Cover design by Andrew Owen

Printed by Stephens & George, Merthyr Tydfil, UK

Contents

1
How We Treat
the Holy Spirit Within

'Your body is the temple of the Holy Ghost which is in you'
(1 Corinthians 6.19).

THE PERSONAL INDWELLING in the believer of the infinite, eternal Holy Spirit is such an amazing blessing and privilege that the mind never wholly grasps it. A daily succession of joys, sorrows, temptations and trials produces various reactions in us, often without stirring our awareness that God is in residence, and that he will be pleased or grieved by what we think, say or do, or that he is ready to help if asked.

The body of every true believer is the property of God, and if it is defiled, either by the entry of worldliness, or by other sinful tastes and desires, the indwelling Spirit is said to be grieved. Writes Paul – 'Grieve not the holy Spirit of God' *(Ephesians 4.30)*, or according to the more striking word order of the Greek, 'Grieve not the Spirit, the Holy One of God.'

How can we so easily lose touch with this awesome, immense fact of spiritual life – that the incomprehensible God takes a place in every redeemed heart, declaring, 'I will never leave thee, nor forsake thee'? The Holy Spirit indwells every Christian from the moment of conversion, so that the inspired Word may say, 'If any man have not the Spirit of Christ, he is none of his' *(Romans 8.9)*. The same passage immediately speaks of Christ being in us, and shows that it is on the Saviour's behalf that the Spirit lives within. Christ indwells, by his Spirit.

Three terms stand out in the New Testament to describe ill-treatment of the Holy Spirit. He may be *resisted*, or *quenched*, or *grieved*, each word describing a level of offence inflicted on our Divine Resident. How easily we forget that he is there, and lose our gratitude to him, our consideration for him, and our dependence upon him!

In his remarkable sermon to self-righteous Pharisees, Stephen, the first martyr, cried – 'Ye do always *resist* the Holy Ghost.' The Greek word means to fall against, such as when one puts one's shoulder to a door to prevent it being opened. To resist is to *oppose* the Spirit. Stephen's hearers resisted salvation, but as believers we may also resist the clear will of God, perhaps by refusing to put away a great sin, or by taking a path of self-indulgence, or by ignoring a clear call of God (in the Word) to take up a spiritual duty or a burden of service. We know what is right, and yet we put our entire weight against the door of obedience, resisting the Member of the Godhead who acts within, the infinitely kind and glorious custodian of our ransomed soul.

It is madness and self-injury to resist the Spirit, so what induces us to do so? Surely it is because we lose touch with the staggering realisation that the Most High God has lodged within, and that it is *his* promptings and urgings that we resist whenever some duty of the Bible is laid on our heart, and we slam shut and barricade the door. Sometimes resisting the Spirit even leads believers to express open opposition to biblical standards (as many Christians do today over the commands to separate from worldly activities).

The second term for offending the Spirit appears in *1 Thessalonians 5.19*: 'Quench not the Spirit.' The Holy Spirit's work is pictured here as a flame of holy conviction or of zeal generated in the heart. Quenching the Spirit suggests the idea of overriding him when he stirs us up to greater service and dedication. He is not violently opposed, as he is when *resisted*, but his stirrings and urgings are suppressed. The mind simply passes over them and moves on. The believer may remain faithful in doctrine, but is no longer so amenable to God in conduct and activity.

The flame or fire produced by the Spirit is love and zeal for the Lord, for the Truth, and for lost souls. It includes conviction of sin when it leads to godly sorrow, indignation against our wrong-doing, coupled with carefulness, vehement desire and zeal to reform. (All these terms are found in *2 Corinthians 7.11*.) The flame of the Spirit may urge us to witness, or to go with compassion to the aid of another person. Do we *quench* the fervour of godly aims kindled in our hearts by the Spirit? Do we quench and suppress the promptings of conscience? Is the maintaining of spiritual zeal sometimes inconvenient, because it is contrary to our mood, or too costly for us? Do we therefore turn away from praise, prayer, thankfulness, dedication and good works?

How can we do this as Christians? Simply by forgetting that it is the ever-present, mighty Spirit of God who is the author of all godly sensations. We do not merely have a divine visitation, which would be wonderful, but something vastly greater – a Divine Resident who ignites the dying embers of spiritual activity, restoring them to full vigour. But we lose sight of the doctrine and the reality of his presence and smother his reviving, energising work within.

The third term describing our insulting treatment of the Holy Spirit appears in *Ephesians 4.30* – 'Grieve not the holy Spirit of God, whereby ye are sealed unto the day of redemption.' This exhortation shows us something of the invisible heart of the Spirit. Surely one of the 'deep things of God' is the revelation that he is grieved, which literally means caused distress and sorrow, by the disrespect and waywardness of believers. Our infinite, all-powerful Divine Resident may be offended, injured and wounded in heart by the indifference of those he is taking to Heaven. The Spirit is grieved when his work in us and for us is ignored. The fact that the invincible, indestructible Spirit may be pained is largely beyond our understanding, but revelation tells us it is so. The Holy Spirit's love for us – like Christ's love – is so great, that he feels for people who are tiny specks of dust before him.

A mysterious question in *James 4.5* asks: 'Do ye think that the scripture saith in vain, The spirit that dwelleth in us lusteth to envy?' This has been more helpfully rendered: '. . . the Spirit who lives in us yearns jealously over us.' With powerful, protective love he grieves over our backslidings and failings, as we do over the mishaps and misfortunes of our own children and loved ones. If only we were more constantly aware of the Spirit's sufferings over us, what a difference it would make to our care and conscientiousness.

Paul seems to have been very aware of his debt to the Spirit, saying, 'I beseech you, brethren, for the Lord Jesus Christ's sake, and for the love of the Spirit . . .' *(Romans 15.30)*. How he loved the Holy Spirit! In this passage he says, in effect, if only we would love the Spirit, we would not grieve him, but pray as never before for the progress of the Gospel. The exhortation to 'grieve not the holy Spirit' is made in the context of holy living, putting off the old person and putting on the new. Corrupt speech is to be curbed, whether boastful, worldly, dishonest, exaggerated, unclean and lustful remarks, or bitterness, gossiping, and hurtful words.

How do we grieve the Holy Spirit? By ignoring the pangs of conscience that the Spirit activates, and failing to check the offensive words or deeds. If we suppress these promptings, and sin regardless, then they will eventually cease, conscience will become dormant, and we will fall headlong into more frequent sinful speech and action, forfeiting communion with God and blessing from him. Similarly, if we fail to pray for and implement active personal kindness toward others, with tenderheartedness and forgiveness, then we grieve the Spirit who works to promote these virtues within us *(Ephesians 4.29-32)*. Once again we must ask, would we not take the stirrings and urgings of conscience much more seriously if we remembered and respected that it is our Divine Resident who works to purify and develop us?

Perhaps it will help if we consider some of the possible reasons why the Holy Spirit is grieved over us. Clearly the first reason for the Spirit's grief is that *he is holy*. Of course the holy One is offended when those he indwells prefer to wallow in things that to him are filth and stench. The altogether pure and holy One stoops to indwell, but we entertain and harbour offensive things in our thought life, to injure him.

The Spirit will also be grieved when we trample on all his past work in our souls. It was the Spirit who opened our hearts to the Gospel by a regenerating act, softening our antagonistic wills, opening our eyes to our spiritual predicament, bringing us under deep conviction of sin, and showing us Christ the Lord as the only Saviour. We then yielded to Christ, and pledged ourselves to him, but now we may pay little heed to the Spirit's continuing shepherding, and in practical terms barely acknowledge his existence.

The Spirit will equally be grieved owing to what Christ has done for us. Who knows more than he and the Father how great a price the Saviour paid for the redemption of each single soul? The eternal, crushing weight of sin was taken by Christ to redeem us, so that he is ours, and he will be our visible King in the eternal glory. But how do we repay him? So often by an inconsistent walk, treating slightly the duty of stirring ourselves to holiness, and sometimes serving our earthly interests with greater fervour than the work of the Lord.

The Holy Spirit is undoubtedly also grieved for *our* sake, because he knows the consequences we bring upon ourselves by neglecting his promptings, such as the loss of assured communion with God, the loss of instrumentality for the Gospel, the loss of response to our prayers, and the loss of deep Christian joy.

Surely, also, the Spirit will grieve because of the blow our lacklustre spiritual walk delivers to the cause of Christ, as younger believers receive from us no example of holiness and zeal, and as watching eyes, especially those of unconverted people around us, see our coldness and inconsistency.

The Spirit is bound to be grieved when the Garden of Eden is replicated in our hearts; when in moments of rebellion we draw back from full commitment to some Christian obligation or duty, thinking to ourselves in words like those of the serpent, 'Has God said there will be consequences?' If pride grows, and self-love increases, or if covetousness gets control, or ingratitude deepens, then the Spirit will grieve over us to a degree we cannot grasp.

In all that we have said here about the promptings of the Holy Spirit, we do not mean to give the impression that the Spirit will reveal things to believers that are outside the Bible. He will not, for example, reveal to us authoritative doctrine, because Scripture teaches clearly that everything we need to know has been revealed once for all in the Book of God. This Bible is the complete, full and sufficient authority for the knowledge of God, for salvation, for the living of the Christian life, and for the operation of churches. All modern claims to fresh information by vision or direct word are totally mistaken.

The Holy Spirit, however, constantly stirs the conscience, reminds us of Scripture, enables us to understand the Bible (if we humbly ask, and use the Bible's own rules of interpretation), clarifies our minds (as we think through issues), and even reminds us of spiritual duties and of other important things that we may forget. Frequently he pours into us immense joy and appreciation of the Word, as we reflect upon its riches. The mighty Holy Spirit, dwelling within, interacts constantly with believers, but never so as to bypass or cause neglect of the infallible Word already revealed by him. The person who says, 'The Lord told me this,' following an imagined inner voice, has wandered far from the standard of the Bible.

The gracious work of the Spirit in believing hearts is also described by Paul in *Galatians 5.16-18*. We are urged to walk in the Spirit, and by so doing to avoid fulfilling the lust of the flesh. There is, says the apostle, a battle in the heart, caused by our residual tendency to sin rising up in desire for gratification, resenting the new nature created by the Holy Spirit. The Spirit, however, opposes these sinful desires 'so that ye cannot do the things that ye would'. He activates the conscience, so that we cannot lightly and easily commit the proposed sinful deed, or say those wrong words. We are pulled up short, and made aware that we are about to offend God. But what if we press past this protecting barrier? What if we sin in spite of the Spirit activating the conscience? It may be a major temptation or a persistent offence, and we *resist* (oppose) the Spirit. It may be, however, that we do not offer any opposition or resentment, but simply *quench* (or quietly override) his promptings. Either way we shall certainly grieve the Spirit.

'If ye be led of the Spirit,' says Paul, 'ye are not under the law,' meaning that the person who is sensitive to the work of the Divine Resident, and conscientiously obeys, may be assured that he is truly saved, and no longer under the condemnation of the law. The law, of course, remains as the ruling moral standard of our lives, but we are no longer to be judged by it, for Christ has taken away its sting.

'If we live in the Spirit,' writes the apostle, 'let us also walk in the Spirit.' Then, being constantly grateful for his kind presence, sensitive to his stirrings, and conscientious in response, we will taste and prove the Spirit's power and blessing, and we shall experience advancing godliness, joy, peace, understanding and usefulness. Resist not his stirrings in the heart, which call to greater commitment and spiritual service. Quench not his urgings nor his movings of conscience. And do not grieve him by neglect.

Finally, resist not, quench not, and grieve not the Holy Spirit by neglecting the facility of prayer and intercession. Do not resist any duty, or quench any urgings, for it is the Spirit who perfects and translates prayer into the language of Heaven, helping our infirmities, making intercession for us with an earnestness far beyond our reach, and conforming our prayers to the glorious will of God *(Romans 8.26-27)*. A remarkable hymn of William Bunting, a nineteenth-century Wesleyan preacher, captures the thoughts of sincere believers in relation to the Spirit, and puts an appropriate response into the heart:

1

Holy Spirit! pity me,
Pierced with grief for grieving thee;
Present, though from sense apart,
Listen to a grieving heart.

2

Sins unnumbered I confess,
Of exceeding sinfulness;
Sins against thyself alone,
Only to Omniscience known:

3

Deafness to thy whispered calls,
Rashness midst remembered falls,
Transient fears beneath the rod,
Treacherous trifling with my God.

4

Tasting that the Lord is good,
Pining then for poisoned food;
At the fountains of the skies
Craving creaturely supplies.

5

Worldly cares at worship time;
Faithless aims in works sublime;
Pride, when God is passing by;
Sloth, when souls in darkness die.

6

O how lightly have I slept
With my daily wrongs unwept,
Sought thy chidings to defer,
Shunned the wounded Comforter.

7

Still thy comforts do not fail,
Still thy healing helps avail;
Patient Inmate of my breast,
Thou art grieved, yet I am blest.

8

O be merciful to me,
Now in longing, Lord, for thee!
Father, pardon through thy Son
Sins against thy Spirit done!

William Bunting, 1805-66

2

The Christian's Personal Struggle
A simplified view of Romans 6 and 7, showing how to
overcome trial and temptation

THREE REMARKABLE CHAPTERS of Paul's letter to the
Romans tell believers how to combat personal sin, beginning
with a graphic description of the problem, and including
an eight-step plan for dealing with temptations. Sanctifying light
streams out of these verses, and once we see it, we will never again
be confused about the way to advance in holiness. This chapter will
take the chief headings of Paul's inspired teaching to give the sense
and the application, rather than all the detail, rich as it is. The next
chapter of this book will look at the eight-step plan.

An illustration at the close of *Romans 5* sets the scene. There Paul
speaks of two reigning monarchs, 'King Sin', on the one hand, and
'King Grace' on the other. Sin was formerly our absolute ruler, but
when, at conversion, grace conquered our lives, sin was emphatically
dethroned. From that time we became *forgiven* people, placed surely
and certainly on the highway to Heaven, safe in the saving, keeping

mercy of God. In the light of this, the opening words of chapter six come as a great challenge to every believer's heart – 'What shall we say then? Shall we continue in sin, that grace may abound?' The key to understanding these words is to get the *scale* right. Some Christians think that Paul has in mind people who commit scandalous sins without care or conscience, presuming on the grace of God to pardon them. This idea, however, has the scale all wrong, because Paul is writing to typical Christians who would not dream of living adulterous lives, for example, or stealing. Paul surely has in mind the sins of heart and mind that continue to be committed by true Christians, saying, 'Shall we be casual about holiness, and rest on the fact that grace will save us anyway?'

The challenge is necessary, because believers are frequently too relaxed about holiness. We tend to lower our guard, allowing ourselves to give way to 'lesser' sins, such as a *little* covetousness, or a *small* measure of selfishness, or a *spot* of peevishness, or a *moment* of pride, or *spasmodic* skipping of devotions. Moods and tempers (though, of course, not too extreme in scale) are allowed to go unbridled, and perhaps 'white lies' and exaggerations also, or fragments of unkind, harmful gossip, and many other slithers and scraps of pre-conversion life.

We may let all these things go unchallenged and unfought, consoling ourselves with the thought that at the end of the day we will repent, and God will forgive us. After all, we think, these are only 'moderate' sins. So we cut corners, permit ourselves a considerable degree of latitude, and become relaxed and complacent about these 'lesser' sins. To us, sin is no longer as dangerous as it was, because we rejoice in the doctrine of final perseverance, so we do not have to worry unduly. It is in the context of these 'ordinary' sins, which gradually take us over, making us deeply offensive to our holy God, that Paul utters the convicting words – 'Shall we continue in sin, that grace may abound? God forbid. How shall we, that are dead to sin, live any longer therein?' How can we do this? – he seems to say.

How shocking, how callous, how ungrateful, that people who have 'died' to the condemnation due to them on account of their sin, and who have 'died' to its absolute reign over them, should continue to wallow in it at any level. If we get the scale right, the words shock us as ordinary Christians.

Paul is warning about the folly of complacency, which discards deep concern for a holy life. 'God forbid!' he says, the Greek meaning – 'Let it never be!' It is the most powerful expression of horror he could use. How can we who are dead to the rule and eternal consequences of sin, allow it to re-establish its grip over our lives?

The two natures of the believer

Then, from *Romans 6.6*, Paul turns to one of the most important aspects of the battle against sin. He begins to explain the apparent contradiction in every believer, namely, that while there is a real longing for holiness, sin still rises up in the heart. Traditionally, reformed expositors have called this the conflict of two natures, the old nature (dethroned and greatly weakened, but still there) and the new nature (an altogether better nature given at conversion). Paul does not actually mention two natures, but they are implied, and provide a most helpful picture of the points he makes. (The nearest he comes to speaking literally of two natures is in *Ephesians 4.22-24*, where he tells believers to put off the old man, which is corrupt, and to put on the new man which God has made in holiness.)

To return to verse 6, the apostle says: 'Knowing this, that our old man is crucified with him, that the body of sin might be destroyed, that henceforth we should not serve sin.' The old nature (the old man), the person controlled by earthly, sinful, selfish aims and deeds, has died. But in what sense has it died? Firstly, it has died as *ruler (Romans 5.21)*, having lost its total, unrivalled, absolute power over the believer. Secondly, it can no longer bring that person down to hell. It has not died, however, in the sense of no longer existing.

Past writers have used various expressions to describe this 'death' of the old nature, saying that the dominion or inevitable mastery of sin is broken at conversion, but it is still there, a humiliated, weakened force, smouldering to reassert itself. King Sin is no longer on the throne, and no longer masters the believer, but he remains as a malevolent force in the form of 'residual sin'. The Christian's ongoing task is to put to death residual sin, a task that will be ultimately and permanently accomplished at the moment of physical death, by the power of God. In the meantime, says Paul, don't continue to serve sin, complying with its whims and urgings, but fight it. This is the meaning of verse 6 – 'Knowing this, that our old man is crucified with him, that the body of sin might be destroyed, that henceforth we should not serve sin.'

The new nature is the *superior*, stronger force in the Christian, while the old is the *inferior* and weaker. The new and the old, therefore, are in no way equal, but the old may triumph over the new when a believer is complacent about godly living.

Is sanctification entirely by faith?

Someone may object to the teaching that the old nature must be fought, believing that sanctification is a work of faith, and God will do it all for us if we trust him. Paul, after all, uses the words – 'Reckon ye also yourselves to be dead indeed unto sin, but alive unto God . . .' *(6.11)*. But Paul does not mean that believers must bring themselves to think that they are immune from sin, in the hope that this will then become a reality. He means that Christians should reckon or count their blessings, reflecting on what Christ has done for them in taking away the condemnation of sin, and breaking its dominion over them. By reviewing these tremendous blessings, believers become indebted to the Lord *(8.12)* and motivated to try harder in resisting temptation. Paul is saying: 'Count your blessings and think of your status as one set free from the eternal consequences of sin! In the light of this, how can you yield or surrender your body or feelings to the service of sin, to be used as weapons in Satan's campaign to promote evil, bring down Christians, shame the Gospel and discredit Christ? On the contrary, consciously yield your lives and conduct to God every day, to be loyal to him alone.' (This is the essence of *Romans 6.11-13*.)

Do we go over to the enemy? Of course, we do not mean to, but we do, by neglect, by failure to rededicate ourselves daily, and by excusing and permitting so many 'little' sins, which steadily grow to be more numerous and serious. If we would only give ourselves every day wholly to the service of Christ, remembering our spiritual status, then sin would not regain its former mastery over us.

In the process of urging believers to take active steps to greater holiness, Paul uses another argument in verse 15, saying that to obey sin is to commit treason. 'Shall we sin,' he asks, 'because we are not under the *[condemnation of the]* law, but under grace? God forbid.' Don't you know, he says, that if you allow yourselves to become servants of sin once again, you will have re-enlisted as sin's servant? You will have gone back to sin, cap in hand, deserting Christ and putting yourself at sin's disposal.

The believer is someone who has taken a stand and pledged himself to Christ (verse 17), receiving a new nature. How can he act

---

ROMANS 6.11-17

11 Likewise reckon ye also yourselves to be dead indeed unto sin, but alive unto God through Jesus Christ our Lord.

12 Let not sin therefore reign in your mortal body, that ye should obey it in the lusts thereof.

13 Neither yield ye your members as instruments of unrighteousness unto sin: but yield yourselves unto God, as those that are alive from the dead, and your members as instruments of righteousness unto God.

14 For sin shall not have dominion over you: for ye are not under the law, but under grace.

15 What then? shall we sin, because we are not under the law, but under grace? God forbid.

16 Know ye not, that to whom ye yield yourselves servants to obey, his servants ye are to whom ye obey; whether of sin unto death, or of obedience unto righteousness?

17 But God be thanked, that ye were the servants of sin, but ye have obeyed from the heart that form of doctrine which was delivered you.

against his promises? How dare we say to ourselves, as we give way to sin, 'It will only be this once; I will vent my anger just this time; I will covet this thing I long for, but I will not go too far.' 'God forbid!' says Paul. How outrageous! You are doing the bidding of sin, and defecting to the enemy's side. Satan will scarcely believe his eyes, and the demons of hell will gloat and sneer.

'Furthermore,' Paul warns in effect, 'do we not realise that smaller sins inevitably lead to greater sins, and there is no defence against this process?' In verse 19 he speaks of how believers previously yielded their bodies 'to iniquity unto iniquity', meaning that there is an unavoidable increase in entanglement with sin.

Finally, the apostle provides extra motivation for holiness by calling Christians to see the fruit within their grasp. Before conversion (verse 21) they had no accomplishments of character – only condemnation – but afterwards, as servants of God, obedience led to advancing holiness, to be crowned by glorification and Heaven. In the light of this outcome, how can believers allow themselves to fall into dangerous slackness over any sin, however small? With eternal life beckoning, and its attainment as sure as the power and promises of God, should they not yield every part of themselves to God (verse 22), seeking *every day* to be honest, unselfish, faithful, humble, sensitive to others, loving, fair, forbearing and gracious?

ROMANS 6.21-22

21 What fruit had ye then in those things whereof ye are now ashamed? for the end of those things is death.

22 But now being made free from sin, and become servants to God, ye have your fruit unto holiness, and the end everlasting life.

In the famous seventh chapter the apostle shows that the law is vital to bring conviction of sin, but is unable to reform the convicted sinner. Before his conversion, Paul's sinful heart twisted the law, making it endorse his lifestyle. Sin spoke to his pride, saying that through keeping the *ceremonial* parts of the law he could become a worthy servant of God. Under this delusion he was blind to the *moral* requirements of the law, so that evil desires could flourish unchecked in his life. With this false view of the law, his real sin went unnoticed, as if it were dead. (This is the meaning of verse 8.)

However, once the moral law convicted him, and his sin 'revived' (in his conscience), he realised with horror that he was condemned to death (verse 9). He then found that the law that was designed to show the way to life (if one could perfectly obey its moral demands) actually condemned him to death (verse 10). Sin, by deceiving Paul into thinking he was keeping the law, slew him eternally (verse 11). There was nothing wrong with the law (verse 12), but sin twisted Paul's view so that he only noticed the ceremonial parts. Once he realised what the law really said about moral behaviour, how he had been deceived, then he saw the exceeding sinfulness of sin, that could even hijack and distort the law to destroy a soul (verse 13). But with conversion everything changed, because Paul then became extremely sensitive to the moral law as his rule for life.

Up to verse 14 Paul has written in the past tense, speaking of his experience before conversion. From this point he speaks in the present tense as a converted man. There can be no doubt that he

---

ROMANS 7.8-14

8 But sin, taking occasion by the commandment, wrought in me all manner of concupiscence. For without the law sin was dead.

9 For I was alive without the law once: but when the commandment came, sin revived, and I died.

10 And the commandment, which was ordained to life, I found to be unto death.

11 For sin, taking occasion by the commandment, deceived me, and by it slew me.

12 Wherefore the law is holy, and the commandment holy, and just, and good.

13 Was then that which is good made death unto me? God forbid. But sin, that it might appear sin, working death in me by that which is good; that sin by the commandment might become exceeding sinful.

14 For we know that the law is spiritual: but I am carnal, sold under sin.

writes now as a believer because he has come to hate sin and deeply regret it (verse 15). He now wants to do good (verse 19); he delights in God's law (verse 22), and he praises God for deliverance (verse 25). This new Paul (so he tells us in verse 25) has two natures, one called his *mind* (the new nature) and the other his *flesh* (the old), and these are involved in continuous conflict.

The second part of verse 14 shocks the reader so much that it seems impossible that Paul could be describing himself as a believer, for he writes – 'but I am carnal, sold under sin.' These words, however, only seem to be impossible as a description of a believer's life if we have in mind the wrong *kind* of sin. As with chapter 6, the key to the passage is to get the *scale* right, because Paul is not thinking about sins such as murder, adultery or extreme uncleanness. He has in mind the standards of the Christian life, where the aim is much higher. He requires in himself *complete* honesty, *total* unselfishness, *complete absence* of pride and self-consideration, *zero* covetousness, *unlimited* kindness, *abounding* love for God, and *complete, unwavering* trust in him in all circumstances. Paul longs to be a person worthy of God's

---

ROMANS 7.15-25

15 For that which I do I allow not: for what I would, that do I not; but what I hate, that do I.

16 If then I do that which I would not, I consent unto the law that it is good.

17 Now then it is no more I that do it, but sin that dwelleth in me.

18 For I know that in me (that is, in my flesh,) dwelleth no good thing: for to will is present with me; but how to perform that which is good I find not.

19 For the good that I would I do not: but the evil which I would not, that I do.

20 Now if I do that I would not, it is no more I that do it, but sin that dwelleth in me.

21 I find then a law, that, when I would do good, evil is present with me.

22 For I delight in the law of God after the inward man:

23 But I see another law in my members, warring against the law of my mind, and bringing me into captivity to the law of sin which is in my members.

24 O wretched man that I am! who shall deliver me from the body of this death?

25 I thank God through Jesus Christ our Lord. So then with the mind I myself serve the law of God; but with the flesh the law of sin.

lovingkindness to him, and entirely yielded up to his service. But even as he longs to attain these wonderful virtues and standards, he finds he falls short of them. He hates his failings, recognising that he still has within him remaining sinfulness, which he calls 'the flesh'. Certainly, this no longer dominates him as once it did, but in reaching for the standard of godliness which he desires, the flesh obstructs him constantly.

This, surely, is the experience of all believers. We want to love souls, to utter only gracious, edifying words, to think only unselfish and good thoughts, to be helpful and sensitive, and to avoid all self-pity and murmuring in times of trial. But we fail the standard so often, and cry out: 'I am carnal, sold under sin. For I do and say and think things that I hate.' Paul frankly admits that he is a divided person (verse 17). His mind demands of himself a godly standard (verse 18) but by himself he lacks the power to accomplish his aim. Failure is not what he wants (verses 19-21), but it is due to the continued presence and drag of a sinful nature.

'I see another law [or principle] in my members,' says Paul, 'warring against the law of my mind, and bringing me into captivity' (verse 23). Ideas come into our minds, and desires enter our hearts as the old nature seeks to recapture some part of us, and to drag us back to laziness, self-consideration, covetousness, self-pity, moaning, grumbling and evil imaginings.

Paul does not mean to excuse himself in any way. He does not speak as though his remaining sin-tendency is not his fault. Whenever he falls short of the mark, he accepts that he is to blame, and he feels it all too keenly. What remains of this old nature within him thwarts his longing for complete holiness (verse 23), and he cries out in anguish (we paraphrase), 'O wretched man that I am! Who shall deliver me from this body that *would have* taken me to death?' The answer is – 'Jesus Christ our Lord'.

Paul will be saved from the continuing influence of his dethroned *old* nature by Christ in three ways:–

(i) Through Christ's work on his behalf he has already received a new nature which greatly prevails over the old.

(ii) Through Christ giving him the Holy Spirit he will receive promptings of conscience, and help to defeat the promptings of the old nature whenever he calls for it.

(iii) Christ will finally call him home to glory and in that moment will purge his old nature away entirely, giving him total and perpetual victory over it.

We have attempted to explain as briefly as possible some of the great verses of *Romans 6-7*. The next chapter traces Paul's positive steps for holiness.

3
Paul's Positive Plan for Holiness
in Romans 7 and 8

NESTLING IN PAUL'S UNFOLDING of the two natures
in the believer is a surprisingly simple eight-stage plan
for advancing in holiness and defeating sin. The first
step appears in *Romans 7.14*, and again in verse 18, and this is the
essential starting point for progress in sanctification:–

1. Recognise the problem

'I am carnal,' Paul acknowledges, adding, 'For I know that in me
(that is, in my flesh,) dwelleth no good thing'. We too must accept
that the remains of the old, fallen nature, although defeated and
subdued, are still within us, and a battle must be maintained against
them. Failure to recognise this will lead to fatal complacency. Failure
to fight will hand dominance back to the defeated old nature.
A serious determination to struggle against sin is the only way to

live as a Christian, yet it is a stance that many professing Christians today, bombarded by worldliness and show-business informality and entertainment, seem unwilling to take. The Christian life is the happiest life on earth, but in the struggle against personal sin we should be deadly serious and highly conscientious. We must recognise and struggle against the 'old man' – our sin tendency.

2. Have positive aims

The second stage in the journey to holiness is found in Paul's words: 'For the good that I would . . .' *(7.19).* 'I would' means – I choose, determine or intend to do. The term indicates a clear mental intention. Without rushing to complete the verse, we see that the apostle has aims or goals in his mind as he embarks upon his day. He does not stroll into it vaguely, devoid of aspirations, but has a clear view of the standards he hopes to honour. This is the outlook of the athlete who trains daily to improve performance, working to achieve certain times or distances. The athlete would be a fool to work without positive targets.

We should ask ourselves – What sort of person must I be today? Surely I must pray, and strive for the fruit of the Spirit. In practical terms I must long and plan to be more patient, more concerned for others (especially their spiritual well-being), more edifying in speech, and more diligent in all that I do. In what areas of life and character do we fail? A practical strategy or plan to succeed in these very areas should be determined in our minds and committed to prayer as we embark on the day before us.

Do we formulate objectives for ourselves regularly, and especially when entering some new phase or location in life? Paul clearly shows his policy of objectives in those words – 'The good that I would,' or 'The good that I consciously and specifically intend.' To omit this daily plan and pledge is to lose half the staircase to the upper floors of the house of holiness.

3. Plan to avoid sin

The third of Paul's stages is found in the second half of verse 19 – 'but the evil which I would not ...' We must again point out the strong note of planned intent in these words, the sense being – 'the evil which I determine or intend not to do'. We are looking at the plan of action in the mind of Paul as he aims *not to do* certain things. He furnished his mind in stage 2 with positive good intentions, and now he commits himself to stand firmly against specific sins. We dare not presume to know exactly what wrongs were in Paul's plan, but we know only too well what should be in our own. Some believers know they fall easily to covetous desires, and they should commit themselves regularly, perhaps daily, to avoiding them.

Some may have yielded to impure thoughts, and each day must now begin with a firm embargo and prayer. Some fall readily into testiness or outbursts of temper, and the aim to resist these at all costs should be uppermost in their daily plan. Some readily blurt out wrong words, perhaps of gossip or boasting or hurt. Some know that their 'demon' is selfishness, others laziness, others untruthful speech ranging from exaggeration to dishonest excuses or worse.

Sin will not be broken and overcome without a longing to avoid it, and the preparation of a prior battle-plan of intentions. In our campaign for sanctification do we with Paul practise this plan-and-pledge stage reflected in the words: 'the evil which I would not ...'?

4. Keep up self-examination

Alongside the positive and negative aims, we find in verse 19 that Paul is acutely aware of his *results* in the struggle for holiness, saying – 'For the good that I would I do not: but the evil which I would not, that I do.' What would be the point of setting aims if we took no interest in how we performed? These matters were so important to Paul that he kept watch and reviewed his conduct, probably every day. He appears in these verses to be deeply concerned and disturbed when his aims are not met, and no doubt repentance and renewed dedication followed. What progress can be made if self-examination is omitted? Naturally, we do not like these moments of shame and pain, but they are not only vital for securing ongoing forgiveness and closeness to the Lord, but they are essential for spurring us on to apply the previous stages. If we leave out these moments of pain and regret, the sin in question will cease to seem serious. If we bypass the daily spasm of shame the conscience will gradually lose its sensitivity. The old hymn of William Bunting quoted earlier laments the neglect of self-examination:–

> O how lightly have I slept
> With my daily wrongs unwept,
> Sought thy chidings to defer,
> Shunned the wounded Comforter.

It is not advisable to spend a long time in review, but we must seek cleansing for all our sin in general, and also for known specific sins in particular, regretting them before the Lord, and remembering them 'in the shadow of Calvary'. Then we should sincerely pledge to avoid them by the help of the Spirit.

Self-examination includes the recognition of our failure to do right (sins of omission), as well as our known wrongdoing (sins of commission). In secular life, what business would survive without awareness of its performance and its finances? Paul's autobiographical words show that he kept a close watch on his walk by self-examination, and so must we.

5. Long for overall improvement

Paul possessed a deep longing to narrow and close the gap between his present condition and the pure standard of Christ, and this is seen in his exclamation – 'O wretched man that I am! who shall deliver me from the body of this death?' (Romans 7.24.) He realises his weakness, and hungers and thirsts after righteousness. This is more than self-examination, which refers to an assessment or review of a person's performance. Self-examination faces the facts, while a longing for improvement stretches forward in the spirit of *Philippians 3.13-14*:

> 'Brethren, I count not myself to have apprehended: but this one thing I do, forgetting those things which are behind, and reaching forth unto those things which are before, I press toward the mark for the prize of the high calling of God in Christ Jesus.'

Paul also shows his longing in the exhortation of *Romans 12.1*:

> 'I beseech you therefore, brethren, by the mercies of God, that ye present your bodies a living sacrifice, holy, acceptable unto God, which is your reasonable service.'

Such a longing is ready to dedicate oneself to God for holiness every day, to wage war against temptation as if life depended on it, to stay clear of circumstances which present temptation, and to particularly guard the mind and its thoughts. This longing to improve is a hatred of sin coupled with a strong desire to please God. It is the spirit of a craftsman seeking perfection, to whom a rough and ready product is something shameful. Do we have this longing? It is often jolted into existence by self-examination accompanied by specific prayer for it.

6. Seek spiritual help

This sixth step for holiness also comes from verses 24-25 of chapter 7 – 'Who shall deliver me from the body of this death? I thank God through Jesus Christ our Lord.' Paul provides the detail in chapter 8 in the exhortations to walk 'after the Spirit' (verses 1 and 4), and to obtain power from the Spirit (verses 11 to 14).

The Lord's Prayer teaches believers to pray: 'Lead us not into temptation, but deliver us from evil.' When wrong desires and tempers rise from the old nature, or when strong temptations come from around us, we call on the Lord. Daily we pray for a lively conscience and a fresh realisation that we are observed by the Lord. Strong and besetting sins yield following earnest prayer, because the Spirit gives power to resist them, often along with a sense of revulsion against the sin.

Much spiritual help comes to believers from reflecting on the arguments the apostle advances in chapters 6 and 7, appealing to their privileges and saying, in effect, 'How can *we* go on in sin?' As we reflect on all that Christ has done to save us from catastrophe and bring us to glory, we are stirred to greater determination in the fight against sin.

7. Mind heavenly things

Another crucial step to advancing in sanctification is the work of actively directing our interests to spiritual matters. This is described in chapter 8 verses 5-6:–

> 'For they that are after the flesh do mind the things of the flesh; but they that are after the Spirit the things of the Spirit. For to be carnally minded is death; but to be spiritually minded is life and peace.'

To 'mind' the things of the flesh or of the Spirit means – to set the mind on either of these things. A parallel text is *Colossians 3.2* – 'Set your affection on things above, not on things on the earth.' Obviously, it is right and healthy to take an interest in many wholesome topics relating to human affairs, but never to major on them in personal reflection to the dwarfing of spiritual things. To mind heavenly things is to be strongly drawn to spiritual study, reading and conversation; to be keenly concerned to hear about Christ's mission in this world, and the blessings and trials of Christian workers everywhere; to be sensitive to the needs and experiences of other believers, so as to include them in our personal ministry of intercession; and to be always praying for vital opportunities to witness and encourage seekers.

If these are the believer's chief interests, temptation will lose much of its appeal and tenacity, and sins such as covetousness will find little opportunity to gain a foothold. The management of interests is a Christian duty that requires a degree of planning, and frequently the redirecting of thoughts and speech when these drift over much to worldly interests. Whatever engages the believer most will shape that person's heart and outlook, in line with the words of Christ, 'For where your treasure is, there will your heart be also' *(Matthew 6.21)*.

8. Mortify sin

Now comes the key action of this series of steps, the mortifying of sin, meaning the terminating of rising sinful desires. Mortification means putting to death these aspirations, and quenching sinful moods, tempers, words and acts. Paul says: 'If ye through the Spirit do mortify the deeds of the body, ye shall live' *(Romans 8.13)*. Not one of the steps may be overlooked, but this eighth is probably the decisive one. Grasping the help of God, by prayer, we put the sin to death and redirect our thoughts to something higher and better.

Over forty years ago my wife and I were engaged in the planting of a new church just north of London, and in the goodness of God had secured a very large area of land for building. The ground was thickly covered by scrub that had ruled for decades. The worst of the tangled mass of wild bushes and thorns was cut down and dragged away by heavy clearing equipment, but the soil remained infected by obstinate roots. How would these be tamed?

The most achievable solution was to buy a heavy, industrial rotary cutter to regularly mow just above the ground, and so turn it into a field of grass. The scheme worked well, and soon the area looked more like a lawn, with little sign of the briars and thorns. For the time being these had been vanquished, but if the regular mowing was missed, horny, tough shoots began to appear again, sounding the alarm that the scrub was still there and could regain control of the ground.

Christians have two natures, a superior, dominant new nature, and a defeated and diminished old nature, but the latter is still there, and the weeds and shoots of the old nature must be cut off the instant they appear. Through regular mowing, the task of managing our church meadow became easier both for machine and operator, but with neglect it became much harder. If the believer allows old sins to develop even a little, giving them free rein only for a while, they will become harder to suppress. A little loss of temper, then a little more, then more vehement outbursts, and in no time the tantrums can barely be controlled. If a believer makes a dishonest excuse or exaggerates something, or tells a few white lies, a steady deterioration will develop which will quickly shatter that person's integrity altogether. If we mortify the deeds of the body every day, the task becomes easier, by the help of the Lord, and the likelihood of falling prey to some great sin becomes increasingly remote. But if we mortify only spasmodically, we subject ourselves to painful work and much failure.

All the steps help greatly

All the steps or stages described here are necessary. In the case of stage 1 – to fail to recognise the problem caused by the remains of the old nature leads to confusion, because you must know who your enemy is and how he fights. In the case of stage 2 – to have no positive aims is unproductive vagueness; and, in the case of stage 3 – to have no aims to avoid specific sins is to bring a flabby, purposeless spirit to a deadly campaign. In the case of stage 4 – to skip self-examination is to allow indifference and self-righteousness to take over the heart. In the case of stage 5 – to have no burning longing to improve is to excuse sin and lose one's awe at the holiness and greatness of God.

In the case of stage 6 – to allow days to pass without calling on God for help in resisting specific sins, is to surrender to them; and in the case of stage 7 – to have greater interest in earthly things than spiritual things is to hand over the mind to spiritual coldness, and to sap vital energy needed for the battle. Finally, in the case of stage 8 – to fail in the active termination of sinful desires and acts, is to make peace with the enemy when victory is within sight.

4
Walking in Spiritual Joy
The Christian's Happiness

'But the fruit of the Spirit is love, joy, peace, longsuffering, gentleness, goodness, faith' *(Galatians 5.22)*.

WHEN THE HOLY SPIRIT first works in our lives, he communicates not joy, but sorrow. He stirs our complacent and indifferent hearts, giving a deep sense of spiritual bankruptcy and need, and enabling us to see ourselves as we would never choose to do – as condemned sinners in the sight of God. He brings us to repentance and faith, and we experience a transforming work in our lives, including the gift of spiritual assurance and happiness. Before this, we only possessed earthly joy, which ebbed and flowed.

Spiritual joy is a deep cheerfulness and gladness of heart. It includes amazing thankfulness, anticipation and a calm spirit. It comes to us as the direct result of knowing Christ Jesus, along with all that he has done for us, and will do, not just in this life, but eternally. Christian joy has a constant property. It can be outwardly eclipsed sometimes by grief or shock, or fear or sin, but nevertheless it is something that abides in the life of the believer. On occasions it may rise to very great heights. It can also flourish in the worst circumstances, coexisting with fierce conflict, disappointment and loss.

Christ has given us a permanent joy, saying, 'Your joy no man taketh from you.' Alongside the most severe setbacks we may always know and rejoice in the purposes of God, and be glad in his great goodness. So the command comes to us, 'Rejoice in the Lord alway,' a command given in the context of troubles. Paul adds – 'Let your moderation be known unto all men,' meaning, let your magnanimity, your sweet reasonableness, or your deep calm be visible to all. He has in view a situation when we are in distress and difficulty, and tempted to react testily, impatiently or despairingly, yet we should at the same time be able to take comfort in the Lord, and rejoice. This is clearly about a joy that has a variety of forms.

At times this gladness is beyond description, called by the apostle Peter, 'joy unspeakable and full of glory' (1 Peter 1.8). Yet, and here is another characteristic, this joy never ceases to be thoughtful, rational and substantial. It is not like taking a drug, or going into a trance. It is not as if we are carried away by some powerful, emotional, manipulating force. It is always thoughtful, and operating in the mind. We know why we rejoice. Furthermore, this joy does not have to be fed by earthly, material, costly things or pleasures. We may have great Christian joy even in poverty. Countless believers through the history of the world have been happy while enduring degrees of privation that we know little about in our modern western world. Earthly joy needs a constant diet of stimulation, and as soon as this vanishes, so does the joy.

Spiritual joy can also be known irrespective of personality. Believers who possess a very serious disposition have joy in a deep inward form, while those who are more extrovert may possess it in the same measure, but in a different hue. It accommodates wonderfully to different personalities.

Qualities and benefits

Before we speak of how joy may be either blighted or developed, let us think of its qualities and benefits. It is undoubtedly a form of worship, as well as being a component. Aside from services of worship, God desires that his children are happy in him, and appreciative towards him, being consciously buoyed up by his love. Christian joy is a continuous and precious act of worship. It is also the vital component of formal worship, psalmists saying, 'Therefore will I offer in his tabernacle sacrifices of joy,' and, 'I went . . . to the house of God, with the voice of joy and praise' *(Psalms 27.6 and 42.4).*

God is not honoured by unhappy Christians. Of course, there are times when there are setbacks in our spiritual warfare or our labours for the Lord, but we must never allow our underlying trust in the Lord, our calm, and our thankfulness for spiritual blessings to be swept away by such things. Among the benefits of spiritual joy is its strengthening power. When the devil attacks and things are going against us, spiritual joy helps us through and gains for us a strength beyond our own.

Another achievement of joy is that it makes us more useful to God, because the witness of a rejoicing person is generally far more effective than the witness of someone with a heavy spirit. When there is gladness in our hearts, this is sensed by people. We hear so many testimonies of unsaved people who became envious of believers because they saw they had a firm hold upon the Lord and upon divine resources, and were happy people. A downcast Christian is also unlikely to have much room in his heart for the souls of others, because gloom turns us in upon ourselves. A rejoicing believer is, therefore, much more useful in the service of the Lord.

Christian joy also delivers us from so many snares of temptation. We are much less likely to be tempted to great covetousness if we are satisfied, rejoicing people. The Christian who loses, little by little, grateful rejoicing in Christ must make up for lost joy with material things, perhaps more possessions, or a bigger home and better car. The road to covetousness begins where the path of joy becomes overgrown and concealed.

How may joy be lost?

How may we lose this joy? Sin, obviously, deprives us of joy, the explanation being easy to see. Although we must take steps to maintain joy, it is essentially a gift given by the Spirit of God, and the Holy Spirit will withdraw it if there is sin. That is why David prayed in *Psalm 51*, 'Restore unto me the joy of thy salvation.' He had sinned, and his assurance and spiritual joy had been withdrawn. Among the sins or 'works of the flesh' listed as opposites of the fruit of the Spirit *(Galatians 5.19-21)* is wrath or anger, which includes angry reactions. These eliminate Christian joy.

If sin has robbed us of spiritual joy, and we have been plunged into spiritual coldness or gloom, it is no use looking for a Christian counsellor. Only God can forgive and restore joy, and he will not allow us to have spiritual joy when there is unconfessed and repeated sin. If, for example, there is unkind anger within marriage, with lack of courtesy, affection and respect, do we think the Holy Spirit will give spiritual joy while these things are allowed, and given free rein?

Nor can spiritual joy coexist with pride. Nor can it live with envy or resentment. Self-pity also causes us to lose joy, because self-pity consumes the entire capacity of human emotions, leaving no room for gratitude, love and joy. Also, when we go about our day allowing self-pity to go round and round in the mind, we forfeit all joy.

A major cause of the loss of joy is the failure to apply faith, a lesson we all learn over the years. We should say, 'This is hard, but I hold on to the Lord; I will bring my situation before him. I will trust him to either lift me over it, or strengthen me through it. I will reflect upon his goodness in time past, and praise and thank him. I will meditate on his promise that "all things work together for good to them that love God"' *(Romans 8.28)*. Instead, however, we cease to think spiritually, and self-pity and misery take over the heart. Faith has failed.

Perhaps the most unnecessary (and disloyal) cause of lost joy is the failure of appreciation and reflection, even when there is no trial. Do we reflect day by day on our privileges, blessings, opportunities and future walking with Christ? Do we reflect on him, and his Word? Or do we take all our blessings for granted? Do we, through the hours of the day, whenever we have opportunity, thank him in any detail for temporal and spiritual blessings? This is a key source of spiritual joy, and we will consider others in a moment.

We have already mentioned worldliness as damaging to spiritual joy. If we let the powerful musical rhythms of this world fill our head, our joy will be physical, biological, earthly and temporary, because spiritual joy shrinks away from sin-based entertainment. We can't have both. Do we keep worldly company? This will surely take away spiritual joy, because (in the words of the *King James Bible*) 'evil communications corrupt good manners' *(1 Corinthians 15.33)*, meaning, 'evil company corrupts good actions, thoughts and feelings.'

How may we increase joy?

The Holy Spirit, who is the source of spiritual joy, conveys it to us by various means. Firstly he places a measure of joy directly into our souls, 'because the love of God is shed abroad in our hearts by the Holy Ghost' *(Romans 5.5)*. Then, as a parent puts food before a child, which the child must take and eat, the Spirit provides sources of joy that we must draw from.

The first of these is worship. As we sing of the attributes of God, directing our adoration to him, we at the same time are filled with comfort and happiness at having such a Lord, Saviour, Guardian and Friend. As we praise God for Calvary, our hearts are melted and filled with love and gladness. Whether we are worshipping with others, or privately, there is nothing more elevating to the soul's happiness than sincere worship. This is the essence of spiritual living.

Repentance, in a strange way, is also a source of deep joy, because the conscience is settled, the burden of sin removed, and we have peace with God, a peace which passes all understanding. 'We also joy in God,' says the apostle, 'through our Lord Jesus Christ, by whom we have now received the atonement' *(Romans 5.11)*. Our Saviour has taken the punishment, our sin has gone, and God will remember it no more. Our conscience has been purged and made clean. These are unparalleled blessings that can only bring great gladness.

Sometimes we are reminded of sins we committed long ago. How terrible that episode was, and the things we did, thought and said! We feel we must repent of them all over again, but we should never do that. We should praise and thank God that when we repented, he forgave. We should allow the memory of past sin to direct our praise and gratitude to the Christ who died for us, bore the consequences, and washed his sinful disciple clean. What relief, wonder and gladness wells up in the heart when we think – 'God took away that guilt and restored me with new opportunities, and by his help I will live to honour and obey him.' Even from repentance comes a form of humble, grateful joy which moves us to guard more firmly against sin. This is authentic spiritual living.

In the exercise of regular reflection there is considerable joy. 'Consider it in thine heart,' said Moses, 'that the Lord he is God ... there is none else' *(Deuteronomy 4.39)*. 'Consider it in thine heart.' Think upon spiritual matters deeply and at length. Study them; weigh them. And this is what we must do, for without this our joy will be limited. Reflection is an appointed source of joy. One may greatly appreciate receiving a gift, say, of flowers, but full pleasure comes from enjoying them once displayed. Give time to reflect on the history of redemption, on the promises of God, and on the great doctrines of the faith. Think, for example, of the doctrine of perseverance. Learn the texts, know them, and be able to turn to them, for these assure us that if we are in Christ none shall ever pluck us out of his hands; we are his now and for ever. Here is an unfailing source of gladness – to reflect on spiritual things. This is spiritual living.

Then there is the amazing facility of prayer. 'Whatsoever ye shall ask in my name,' said the Saviour, 'that will I do, that the Father may be glorified in the Son' *(John 14.13).* We will not usually ask for material things just for ourselves (except in real need), but if we have in our minds such things as the blessing of others, the proclamation of the Gospel, the help and support of workers for Christ, and our own sanctification, then our prayers will surely be answered. With such a promise from our Lord should we not be happy, glad, and rejoicing people? God himself has said that he will hear our every cry, and respond in his wisdom, his chosen way, and in his time.

We have the incomprehensible privilege of having power to prevail with the sovereign God, and he may yield to our cries, because we are his children and he loves to do so. In the great mystery of his will, he heard our prayers before the foundation of the world, and with the smile of a father, in his own sovereign purpose, he determined to favour with divine consideration even our requests. That is an astonishing privilege beyond human understanding. Can we be gloomy, pessimistic people?

If someone told us he had the ear of the Prime Minister, we might well wonder whether that amounted to much. But if someone says, 'I have the ear of the most high God,' that is an amazing privilege. We need never be crushed or defeated by any situation. We may intercede for someone we love, someone who will not turn to Christ, and who seems to fill his or her head with increasing doubts and antagonistic thoughts as the years go by. But we can say to ourselves, 'The God to whom I pray is the God who determines all things, and so, my rebellious loved one, you may think what you like, but if God hears my prayer, you will be changed, because he is a sovereign God.' Such thinking gives joy and peace in believing.

Equally, we may take to the Lord all our deepest sorrows and burdens. This is yet another priceless privilege, that we can share with the Creator God, the Ruler of Heaven and earth, our sorrows and griefs and burdens, knowing that he cares for his people *(1 Peter 5.7)*. To have these blessings is to have greater riches than the most powerful and wealthy people of all history.

And are we so careless that we forget an answer to prayer the very next day or within a week? Many of God's answers we should diary and deeply inscribe in our memories so that we can review them often, because answers to prayer are astonishing. Do they not come almost hour by hour, day by day, week by week? Sometimes we pray for someone for months, even years, until our prayers for that person begin to fade, and then the prayer is answered. Are we moved for more than a day? Do we not count these things as glorious? The God of Heaven and earth intervenes in my life, hears my faltering ministry of intercession for others, and people are delivered from an eternity of hell, and brought into the kingdom of love and light. These things are stupendous matters, and they lift up our hearts to God in thankfulness, adoration, and happiness. This is true spiritual living, not foolish claims to special gifts, or the imagining of spiritual voices and messages.

Here is another great source of rejoicing – the exploration of the Word. It is a sad thing if my Bible reading is limited to five verses a day, accompanied by shallow consideration. O dear friends, let us read the Word. If you have no other help, read Matthew Henry's commentary to stimulate thought, and let him show you how to read it, and how to delight in it. 'I will delight myself in thy statutes,' says the psalmist, 'Thy law is my delight' *(Psalm 119.16, 174)*. Can we say that?

Even the structure of the Bible is powerful, and a source of joy. For instance, all the New Testament doctrines of grace are to be found in the book of *Genesis*, proving the unity of the Bible, and its divine authorship. Let us spot them, recognise them for ourselves and thank God for them every time we see them. Love the Word of God, its astonishing depths, and its wonderful consistency. Every day ask – What doctrine do I learn here? What reproof do I find? What duty and encouragement and promise is presented? And is my Lord and Saviour in the passage?

Christ is the mighty backbone or cable running right through from *Genesis* to *Revelation*, and there are so very many deep observations and insights into human nature and behaviour in every historical passage. If we look carefully, we will see them. Here is the highest imaginable learning and wisdom, the Book of God, the divine Word, and we have been anointed to enter in, and to grasp it. Let us give thanks, smile and rejoice at every understanding gained. This is spiritual living.

Then we could point to the enjoyment of Christian character, the very handiwork of God, that we see in other believers. We sometimes have cause to grumble about each other. We shouldn't, but we may have cause, because we still all bear the scars of the Fall. Nevertheless, towering above all causes of complaint, we should be moved by the work of grace in other Christians. Look at some Christians, and marvel at their evenness of bearing and thought, their depth of character, their strengths, their unfailing godly reaction to difficulties, their persistent kindnesses, and their grace and courtesy. They were not always like this. This is the touch of Jesus Christ our Lord and Saviour. If only we could all be more like such Christians. We love them, because we see Christ manifested in them, and we are confirmed in our faith, and rejoice.

And how we love to be together, because we have so much in common, and true filial bonds. We largely think the same way, share the same tastes for spiritual things, have the same objectives, love the same things. We talk in spiritual language to each other, and we don't have to explain ourselves. We are never stabbed in the back by each other, and so we may walk in trust. What a wonderful thing it is to be able to take joy in Christian character! How greatly King David valued the godly, so much indeed that he says in *Psalm 141*, 'Let the righteous smite me; it shall be a kindness.' That is how it is when we derive joy from the accomplishments of Christ, even in one another. Truly, 'we know that we have passed from death unto life, because we love the brethren' *(1 John 3.14)*. This is spiritual living.

We may also derive joy from creation around us. This is something we lack in London, living in a heavily built-up city where senses are somewhat dulled. But when we do have opportunity to see natural wonders, we should pause and rejoice in them. We think of David as a boy and as a young man, looking after sheep. We read of him at night looking into the liquid depths of the sky, observing God's creation and saying, 'When I consider thy heavens, the work of thy fingers, the moon and the stars, which thou hast ordained; what is man?' *(Psalm 8.3-4.)* Mankind shrank in David's estimation as he gazed into the vastness of the universe, and the wonders of the heavens. 'The works of the Lord are great, sought out of all them that have pleasure therein' *(Psalm 111.2)*.

We ought to be among those who take pleasure in the works of God. If you are somewhere beautiful, pause, take it in, and reflect. There are certainly ugly things in the world, evidences of the Fall, and even these things confirm our understanding of the Bible, but there are also astonishingly beautiful places. Just admire them, worship God, and say, 'This is my Saviour's handiwork.' Then wonder what it will be like when we soar into the future realm and see the uninhibited marvels of our Creator. Why, the most wonderful scenes in this present world are nothing to be compared with what will be seen everywhere in the eternal glory. So don't rush by, but learn more and more to value every wonder of God's power, for Scripture says these are a source of pleasure and joy to admirers of the Lord. This, also, is spiritual living.

We remember again that trials bring joy. The earliest epistle of the New Testament is most probably that of James, who was pastor at the great church of Jerusalem for thirty years, and the very first exhortation comes in these remarkable words: 'My brethren, count it all joy when ye fall into divers temptations' (meaning trials). Why should troubles and difficulties be a source of *all joy*? Because through them we prove the Lord as at no other time. He sees us through, and we bless him and praise him as he answers our trusting prayers. To derive gladness even from trials is true spiritual living.

We have reviewed major sources of spiritual joy which make us pleasing to God, strengthen our witness, and keep us through all temptation. We should never forget that the supreme source of joy is reflection upon Christ himself. We may and do reflect on the Father, but the Father has perfectly revealed himself in the Son, who is God manifested in the flesh, and so we see the very heart of the Godhead in Jesus Christ our Lord. We see Christ with the eye of faith, making intercession for us in the heavenly places, planning our lives and planning our future. And we can say with conviction, feeling, and great happiness, 'He is the Lord of glory, the Creator of all worlds, the judge of all the earth, the author and finisher of our faith, the land-lord of the universe, and *I am his, and he is mine.*' Could anything in earth or sky or sea be more moving than this? Should we not be filled with happiness and gladness and joy? This is spiritual living.

5
Feeling the Presence of the Lord
Ways in which Christ is Near to his People

'The secret of the Lord is with them that fear him' *(Psalm 25.14)*.

HOW EXACTLY DO BELIEVERS sense the presence of the Lord in their lives? Many passages of Scripture refer to a close union with Christ, including *Ephesians 3.19* where Paul prays that believers may 'know the love of Christ, which passeth knowledge', and that they may be 'filled with all the fulness of God'. In the *Psalms* a wide variety of expressions describe the closeness of the Lord. *Psalm 140.13* speaks of how the upright shall dwell in the Lord's presence, and *Psalm 91.1* breathes wonderful intimacy in the promise – 'He that dwelleth in the secret place of the most High shall abide under the shadow of the Almighty.' In his hour of repentance, David prayed: 'Cast me not away from thy presence' *(Psalm 51.11)*. *Psalm 25.14* has the striking expression 'the secret of the Lord' to describe union with God. The Hebrew word for 'secret' refers to a close-knit gathering or a 'session'. It suggests an exclusive group of people relating confidentially together, and so it depicts the closeness which a Christian has with the Lord.

All this raises a problem, for how is this closeness to be sensed? Some, especially newer believers, are anxious about this question, and this makes them vulnerable to the mystical and sensational ideas of the charismatic movement, and to the imagined experiences of 'pietist' and 'higher life' teachers. What, then, is this secret presence or closeness of the Lord? Is it a feeling? This is a question we have to ask. And if it is a feeling, what kind of feeling is it – a touch, perhaps, or a tingling, or some strange sensation?

The answer to the last question is that it is not a feeling. We must qualify this at once, because anyone who loves the Lord and experiences his interventions in life, and who reflects on him, will experience strong feelings of happiness, gratitude and gladness. Believers feel very deeply as they consider the things of the faith, but their actual union with the Lord is not perceived by feeling.

Many earnest Christians have picked up this idea that they ought to be able to feel something, and it is therefore worth repeating that our devotions will frequently produce immensely strong feelings of assurance and gladness, but these come as a *response* to our grasp of God's goodness, and are not a sensing of his presence. We cannot have any *tangible* feeling, for the simple reason that we know God's presence in our lives *by faith*, and this chapter will seek to show how this works to our blessing.

Some people think that they feel the presence of God when spiritual ideas pop into their head. They think that imagined leadings, visions and words of knowledge springing into their minds are evidence of the Lord's presence. All this is mistaken, and may sometimes be a form of proud spiritual elitism. They are no indication of the presence of the Lord. We know the presence of the Lord *by faith*.

Does this mean that throughout my Christian life I could be deluded about my spiritual standing? If all I know of the presence of God is by appreciating him by faith, could I at the end find I was in error? No, because although I do not sense him by tangible feeling, faith makes him utterly certain to me, and my faith is further confirmed by the wonderful things that he does in my life. We should never say, 'But how can I believe if I cannot get a felt sensation, a tingling, or just something to provide an unmistakable, supernatural sense of his nearness?' We do not need such things, for there is almost a tidal wave of evidence flowing through the life of the one who believes in him, trusts him, and firmly remembers that he is there.

To develop our certainty and enjoyment of Christ's nearness *by faith*, what should we think about? The following observations attempt to answer that question.

In what sense is the Lord near to us? First, the concept of nearness tells us that *we are in his view*. He watches us all the time, and this is a powerful thought. He is near us in the sense that he views us at very close quarters, and fondly, because he loves his people. By faith we know he watches us constantly. We cannot feel his presence, or see him literally, but we know that he is watching, because the Scripture teaches us so. He knows our situation through and through. Whatever happens to us, all is known to him. He permits things to happen and helps us as we call upon him. To reflect on this daily is to know by faith that he is there, and to be mightily comforted and strengthened.

This realisation also increases our zeal for holiness, because if we truly grasp that he sees us at close quarters, we become troubled about our sin, for he sees it all. The biggest curb upon godlessness in Christian people is this daily realisation that the Lord is, as it were, standing right nearby and observing everything we do, not only with his kindly gaze, but also with a disciplinary frown. Imagined spiritual voices and messages never helped anyone to make progress in character and behaviour, but to grasp Christ's nearness *by faith* has a strong curbing, moulding effect.

Secondly, the concept of nearness teaches us that Christ is near in the sense that it is easy to speak to him. Is his presence a touch or a feeling? No, it is the knowledge that he hears every prayer we utter, including every thought, and is able to respond immediately. We do not pray to a God who is a million miles away but to One who knows our situation as though standing alongside us. Nor do we speak to the air. We cannot see him, and we may not visualise him, but the very idea of his closeness helps us to pray, and it also helps us to pray in a right spirit, remembering not to be selfish, but to intercede much for others. He is right beside me – so I *must* ask aright.

Thirdly, the nearness of the Lord also reminds us of our security and protection, guaranteed by him. How can I ever fall as a child of God? How could I be disastrously, eternally swept away? It is shamefully true that I will sin and dishonour the name of Christ, but he is near and will not let me fatally fall. He may discipline and punish me severely, nevertheless he will bring me back. This is not to be seen as an encouragement to sin, because the discipline of the Lord can be very painful, but what a security it is to think that he, in his nearness, notes every transgression and departure, and directs the processes of reclamation and restoration.

Fourthly, we may perceive the nearness of Christ from the doctrine of his making constant intercession for his people *(Romans 8.34; Hebrews 7.25)*. It almost overwhelms the imagination to think that he has us on his heart and in his view every moment in order to intercede on our behalf to his heavenly Father. Is the intercessory work of Jesus Christ merely occasional or periodic? No, it is constant, as he speaks for us through the perpetual vigour of his perfect offering and atoning death, showing his wounds and holding his people in eternal life. All the time, he knows those whom he represents.

Fifthly, we perceive his nearness from the fact that Christ trains his people constantly. They are those who are 'sanctified in Christ Jesus', who is made unto them 'sanctification' *(1 Corinthians 1.2 and*

30). Though he works by his Spirit, yet he also is closely involved. A sportsman cannot be trained unless his coach is present, watching his every move, detecting what he does incorrectly, and sketching out fresh approaches to accomplish his objective. The coach must follow every movement, analysing, correcting and encouraging. This serves as an illustration of the nearness of Christ in the training of his own.

He designs situations to strengthen us and to bring out trust, prayer and forbearance. He beholds each one and says, 'This child of mine needs more patience, or compassion, or understanding, or boldness.' Like a heavenly, personal coach he views us, developing our graces and also training us in witness and service for his glory. As with sportsmen, none may have the benefit of this training, even though saved, if they are not committed Christians, willing to co-operate and develop. Once again we must state that the nearness and presence of the Lord is not a feeling, but an appreciation of what 'nearness' involves, in terms of what he does for us.

Sixthly, the abiding presence of the Lord is evidenced whenever we are prompted by his Spirit, either by a stirring of the conscience, or by being reminded of scriptures or good works or vital duties which we may have lost sight of. This is not to suggest that Christ speaks to us by way of revelation. As we have already pointed out, there is no more revelation, for all the authoritative Truth of God is contained in his Holy Word. A prompting of the Spirit reminds us of matters already revealed.

Frequently the Lord stirs the mind and puts some otherwise forgotten thing into view, but he does not communicate authoritative Truth, except to remind us of what we have learned from the Word. He does, however, help us in all our ways as we look to him. He can and does intervene in our circumstances. The concept of nearness is reinforced by his goodness in so doing.

Seventhly, the concept of the Lord's nearness includes his work of conviction, mentioned in previous paragraphs and in chapter two.

When temptation comes and we begin to yield to it, the alarm is sounded, so that a chord is struck within the conscience, and we know that we should not do that thing. Christ's nearness keeps the conscience lively and reactive. Of course, if we do not co-operate with the stirrings of conscience but rush wilfully on, then he may withdraw his kindly cautions and allow us to plunge into sin, pain, loss, discipline, and sad regrets. But if we look to him to help us in the walk of holiness, he is near enough to put that precious warning touch upon us whenever we are about to go wrong. The concept of nearness is confirmed by the close interaction of Christ with his people in the pursuit of holiness.

Eighthly, the nearness of the Lord is substantiated as we read the Scriptures or reflect on his works. Christ, by his Spirit, touches our minds and brings light and life. He amplifies our understanding, and our hearts are strangely warmed as a better grasp of some matter dawns. Often as we go through our day, the Lord brings a scripture into the mind, because he is always ready to deepen our appreciation of spiritual things. Obviously, we must be 'into the Scripture' as daily Bible readers, loving the Word, for Christ to touch our hearts and bring the meaning home to us. As he brings the Word to life, we know that he is near.

Ninthly, the nearness of the Lord is seen in his engagement with us in his service. If we speak to an unconverted person, what can we achieve? We cannot turn the stubborn will and melt the stony heart. But as we speak, because Christ is near, he frequently works in the heart. We do not have to wait for him to come, for he is ever at hand, and he can make our words effective, using our testimony. If we are trying to help or comfort some fellow believer, how can we be sure that our words will prove a blessing? Christ is near, and he applies them to the understanding and the heart and makes them helpful. The work of Christ, by his Spirit, is a powerful assurance of his constant nearness to his people.

It is such a shame that some believers miss the real meaning of the language of nearness, and interpret it to refer to tangible sensations and voices. Not content to have Christ by faith they long to feel an unmistakable touch, or hear an audible sound.

I remember a lady some forty years ago who would demand to know – 'Do you feel the presence of the Lord?' She once said that she had been to the wedding of an unconverted couple held in a civil register office, and insisted that she had felt the touch and presence of God most remarkably in the God-free ceremony. It is sad when Christian people speak like this, because they miss so much. We know the Lord's presence not by some transient touch or sensation, but by remembering the aspects of his nearness. Then, whether we are unemotional people or the most excitable in the world, we are greatly strengthened and uplifted by the realisation that our Lord is with us.

How may I be sure that the Lord will perform all the activities just listed for me? The answer is given in the psalm: 'The secret of the Lord is with them that fear him; and he will shew them his covenant.' The promise is conditional. Although Christ is always near in the sense that we are never out of his sight, he will not always act towards us as though he were present. He will not always restrain our troubles, keep us from falling into sin, intervene in our lives, answer our prayers, train us, prompt us, convict us of sin, give us assurance, give light on the Word, or even use us. All these activities are conditional, and the condition is – 'The secret of the Lord is with them that *fear* him.' We must fear and obey him. We must reverence and respect him. The psalmist also says – 'Yea, let none that wait on thee be ashamed: let them be ashamed which transgress without cause.' Clearly we must also be serious about holiness if we want to enjoy the activities encompassed in the concept of nearness.

Another condition is, 'Lead me in thy truth, and teach me: for thou art the God of my salvation; on thee do I wait all the day.' We must take guidance seriously. We must not flit through life as though we are free to do whatever we like, but should always remember we are bound to seek God's guidance in all our major decisions.

It is a tremendously elevating experience to see Christ near *by faith* day by day. We get up in the morning, go out to our business, and say to ourselves, 'Christ is near to me; he is watching me with great affection; he is ready to intervene in my affairs; he knows everything that is going to happen to me; he is ready to answer my prayers; he is so near he can do anything that is needful instantly; he will train me and strengthen me for trials; he sees everything, and I will therefore please him, honour him, and love him.'

Are there not such things as 'elevated spiritual experiences' for the believer? Yes, indeed, but these are the times referred to earlier, when the Holy Spirit, perhaps as we read the Word, pray or meditate, so fills our minds with increased understanding and appreciation of Christ's goodness and love, that we are lifted up in happiness, gratitude and wonder.

The presence of God is not a feeling but a realisation, a belief, a conviction which sees and values the implications of the concept of nearness. This is one of the most wonderfully rewarding beliefs of the Christian life. To remember and value these 'ministries' of Christ to his people is worth ten thousand strange sensations. Surely we should pray daily that the Lord would bring the wonders of Christ and his work into view, and write them on our hearts and minds. Then, by faith, we shall know his nearness.

6
The Purpose of our Walk
The Battle for Souls

YEARS AGO WE USED TO SAY that we are 'saved to serve', but that little maxim is out of fashion today. It is, however, biblical and right. This chapter is intended as a call to the tremendous work of the great commission of Christ to his disciples in every age – the gathering in of lost souls. At first sight this topic may not seem to relate to the personal spiritual life, but a believer whose mind and heart is not engaged in Christ's cause cannot expect to make personal spiritual progress, for did not the Lord say, 'Herein is my Father glorified, that ye bear much fruit; so shall ye be my disciples.' Also, he said, 'I have chosen you, and ordained you, that ye should go and bring forth fruit' *(John 15.8, 16)*. It is for this cause saved people are left in the world, and the purpose of all spiritual strength and experience is to equip us for the work.

The battle for souls is a topic which should grip the minds and hearts of all Christians, unless we have become cold and self-contented in spirit. The question behind this chapter is: Do we reflect the martial language of evangelism in the New Testament, and see ourselves as being on a war footing for the souls of men and women? Do we resemble our forebears, especially those of the early church, or of times of reformation and awakening, or any other period of strong church growth?

Tragically, it must be said that reformed Christians today do not often appear to be engaged in a battle for souls. In churches that believe the doctrines of grace it is all too rare for distinctive, dedicated, persuasive evangelistic messages to be heard, and to find really serious labour on the part of church members to reach neighbourhoods. The result of this has been a steady decline of congregations, so that now panic has set in, many reformed churches turning cap-in-hand to the 'seeker-sensitive' churches and saying – in effect – 'Show us how to revive our churches; show us your contemporary praise culture and worship songs. Let us incorporate these into our worship.' Well-known reformed figures are leading the way into a new world. For years they have been ultra-Puritans, and suddenly they have become like charismatics. The power of panic is remarkable.

In the following paragraphs we shall draw encouragement from a number of Bible passages using the language of warfare as a figure for winning the lost to Christ. This, we believe, is the missing factor among many reformed believers. Making soulwinning a central theme will restore vitality and purpose to personal spiritual lives.

Warfare is about militant advance; the prosecution of a vigorous, unrelenting campaign to take territory. Lacking this driving determination, pivotal and historic conflicts have been lost, such as in 1940, when Italy came into the war on the side of Germany. Mussolini spoke haughtily of initiating a 'drive to the Nile', and sent a massive force of five heavily-equipped divisions to the border of Egypt, which was defended by British and Indian troops. The Italian commander, Marshal Graziani, gave the order to this huge force to move forward. The Allies, having little more than two divisions at their disposal, were heavily outnumbered, while in the air the Italians had a five-to-one superiority over the RAF.

General Richard O'Connor, the British commander, was puzzled when the Italian army, having rolled forward 50 miles, suddenly stopped. Reconnaissance officers crept forward and saw through their binoculars an astonishing sight. Hundreds of Italian engineers and labourers were busy digging in and erecting long-term fortifications, even laying a great pipeline for water. One lieutenant radioed back – 'It looks as though they have settled here for ever.' The drive to the Nile had ground to a halt.

General O'Connor was eager to strike, and moved quickly. Early in the morning, as the sun came up, British and Indian forces attacked with maximum impact, finding all the Italians in bed except sentries, and the cooks preparing breakfast. The battle lasted under two days, Allied tanks and infantry prevailing with ease. More than 20,000 Italian soldiers were taken prisoner, along with (as the war historians love to tell us) countless bottles of wine and mountains of spaghetti.

What was the problem that halted the Italian offensive? It was their commander, Marshal Graziani. He would not fight. He moved his enormous army forward, vacillated and dug in, and it cost him, ultimately, his entire army.

How like our British constituency of reformed churches this is! We have fellowships throughout the land equipped with the Word of God and the great doctrines of the faith. We have an abundance of food (fine sermons preached in our pulpits), a superb heritage of example (in our history), and we look after our troops (church members), but so many of our churches are not moving. Where is the thirst for victory? Where is the evangelistic endeavour? How similar we are to a stationary army, and yet we are supposed to be the 'church militant'. The warfare illustration has tremendous suggestive power for the stance and vigour of Bible-believing churches, and we naturally want to know how prominent this theme is in the Bible. After all, if it is set forth as a standard for us, we are bound to be shaped by it, both as individuals and churches.

The martial texts of the New Testament apply to the work of the ministry in general and to evangelism in particular. If we can show that this is so, then as believers we are bound to strive with 'military' zeal in the reaching of souls. *1 Corinthians 9.7*, for example, employs battle language to describe ministers, Paul saying, 'Who goeth a warfare any time at his own charges?' We know that the warfare here includes soulwinning because Paul mentions planting a vineyard, an obvious figure for evangelism. In *2 Corinthians 5.18-20* and *6.4-10* Paul lists the rigours which commend a person serving in the ministry of reconciliation, mentioning various actions, and saying – 'By the armour of righteousness on the right hand and on the left'. This refers to a Roman soldier with his shield in one hand and his attacking sword in the other. Does this resemble our evangelistic stance today?

In *2 Corinthians 10.3-5* the apostle uses very remarkable language: 'For though we walk in the flesh, we do not war after the flesh: (for the weapons of our warfare are not carnal, but mighty through God to the pulling down of strong holds;) . . . bringing into captivity every thought to the obedience of Christ.'

These words may properly be applied to the believer's battle for holiness, but they are intended to apply even more to the battle for souls. Paul is actually defending himself against those who said he was not an apostle, but to do this he mentions the great principles of militant evangelism to which he was committed.

In *1 Timothy 6.12* Paul says to Timothy: 'Fight the good fight of faith.' Is he referring to personal holiness or evangelism? Obviously both, because Timothy received a two-part charge in these epistles, firstly to promote sound doctrine, and secondly to do the work of an evangelist. We are to see both ministries as a battle, and conduct them with great effort.

The language of military action continues in *2 Timothy 2.3-4* – 'Thou therefore endure hardness, as a good soldier of Jesus Christ. No man that warreth entangleth himself with the affairs of this life; that he may please him who hath chosen him to be a soldier.' We know that Paul is thinking of evangelism as well as preaching to the saints because he immediately speaks of enduring 'all things for the elect's sakes, that they may also obtain the salvation which is in Christ Jesus'.

What could be more martial than the picture of Christ in *Revelation 6.2*: 'And I saw, and behold a white horse: and he that sat on him had a bow; and a crown was given unto him: and he went forth conquering, and to conquer.' Here, surely, is the battle for souls illustrated under the direction and leadership of Christ himself.

The longest warfare passage in the epistles is in *Ephesians 6*, beginning – 'Put on the whole armour of God.' Much of the armour is defensive, and clearly represents the believer's struggle against temptations, trials, and attacks that are made on the Truth. However, the offensive sword, the Word of God, is also there, and Paul proceeds to appeal for prayer that he may open his mouth boldly to make known the Gospel as 'an ambassador in bonds'.

We see in *Ephesians 6* the fourfold battle of the Christian church: *the battle for the Truth* (to educate God's people and to defend the faith); *the battle for holiness* ('having on the breastplate of righteousness'); *the battle for assurance* ('taking the shield of faith' to 'quench all the fiery darts of the wicked'); and *the battle for souls* (having 'your feet shod with the preparation of the gospel of peace'). The last of these is certainly not the least, but of prime importance, because it comes first in the great commission given by the Lord. All these activities are described using the language of warfare.

Commendably, the *battle for Truth* is taken very seriously by most reformed preachers today, because we stand for the Reformation, and for the great 17th-century reformed confessions with their remarkable statements of biblical doctrine. Everywhere reformed pastors seek to teach the doctrines with sincerity and diligence.

The *battle for holiness* is also urged by numerous reformed preachers. Godly living and the mortification of sin by the power and help of the Spirit is strongly set forth in numerous pulpits. Does not the reformed tradition have its Puritans with their great expertise in presenting the standards and methods of holiness? We are inevitably concerned to promote and apply these.

The *battle for assurance* received renewed attention from the 1950s, when the notable Dr Martyn Lloyd-Jones and others focused minds once again on Satan's offensive to take away the believer's joy and peace in believing, and how he should be countered. It is vital that these three aspects of the spiritual warfare continue to receive constant and careful attention, but what about the *battle for souls*? Without doubt, this is the one which has faltered and failed during our 'watch', and so much so that there often appears to be no battle at all.

We know well that there are ministers and workers struggling against the trend, and their labours must be acknowledged, but since the 1950s evangelism has been the weakest theatre of war for reformed churches in Britain. Generally speaking, we no longer thrill to the language of Bishop Ryle, who would speak of attacking the strongholds of Satan to rescue perishing souls, and of hunting the fox of unbelief to its lair. Martial language has become an embarrassment.

Dare I mention another military analogy, this time from the American Civil War? At the outset, the Confederate army in the south had fairly bleak prospects against the superior Union forces, but then there was the strange, strange case of General George McClellan. It is said that if this general had speedily marched his huge army of 168,000 men south and taken Richmond (the Confederate States' capital) there might have been an early end to the war. McClellan was the man of the hour, a wealthy former railway chief who exuded decision and authority. When they painted his picture he struck a perfect

Napoleonic stance, even with his hand in his coat. His manual on the art of war was essential reading for officers.

In the winter of 1861-2 his was the best supplied and best fed army ever seen in America, chickens and equipment in abundance arriving in wagons every hour. The trouble was not the availability of recruits and provisions, but the celebrated general. He just wouldn't move. He fussed and hesitated for months, while Abraham Lincoln paced his Washington study in exasperation saying, 'What have we got to do to get him to fight? Why won't he go forward?' Despite a three-to-one majority of troop numbers, McClellan repeatedly appealed for reinforcements and additional supplies, having convinced himself the enemy were far more powerful than they were (or ever could have been). Eventually he did move forward and mount attacks, but these were all too little too late, and much blood shed on both sides accomplished nothing. As a result the noble general went further into his shell until relieved of his command.

Is this not just like our reformed scene? As we mentioned in the case of our earlier military illustration, we are so well equipped, having the Word of God together with many able preachers, and people willing to operate Sunday Schools and visit homes if only churches would organise such activities, yet little or nothing is attempted. We wonder if the angels in Heaven look down and say, 'What have we got to do to get these British reformed Christians to fight? They do not seem interested in the battle for souls.'

We rightly have our obligation and concern for the other theatres of war we have listed, but why not for soulwinning? In this respect we have nothing in common with the Reformers, the Puritans, the preachers of the golden age of Baptist church expansion, the Victorian pulpit, the likes of Whitefield, Carey, Spurgeon and so many others of the reformed school. We have preachers who believe in the free offer of the Gospel, but hardly ever proclaim it. They are mainline Calvinists in theory, but hyper-Calvinists in methodology, for their level of Gospel activity is often no greater.

We have reformed churches with no children's Sunday Schools, no active community visitation, no stress on the necessity of a serving church membership, and no evangelistic preaching. But this is not authentic, historic reformed Christianity. It is something abnormal, and we need to recognise this. Today, maintaining the army takes up all the attention of reformed preachers and writers, while the *purpose* of the army has been all but forgotten. Endless reformed conferences and publications exclusively emphasise *other* departments of the Christian warfare, seemingly unaware that modern British Calvinism has by this omission become disfigured and unsound. As a result, individual believers in many churches have forgotten how to serve the Lord in a corporate way. Are we among them? Do we need to stir ourselves to action?

Earlier in this chapter we asserted that war requires *advance*, and a vigorous prosecution of that aim. If we may add another observation, it is the need for an *intelligent strategy* in warfare. In the battle for souls we need to apply our minds to how we may reach our community, thinking about children, young people and adults.

Unsound church-growth authors have suggested many novel plans, most of which are unbiblical and misguided. Popular ideas today include the abandonment of challenging preaching, the stifling of any mention of sin, the constant use of drama as the premier mode of communication, and the emphasising of worldly entertainment-style music. As we have noted, we are amazed to see these methods favourably considered by some reformed churches that turn in panic to superficiality.

In our reformed circles, however, we often have no strategy or battle-plan at all. In fact, some seem to have the idea that if we hold to the doctrines of grace, it is unsavoury to have campaign objectives of any kind. Some say that the only strategy for soulwinning is to promote holy living among believers, and a very beautiful phrase has come into vogue, namely – 'We believe in the evangelism of holy living.' Of course we do, but the way the phrase is often used really means, 'We believe in doing nothing.'

Certainly, the gracious lives of Christian people will attract others, but this is only a part of the battle for souls. Nevertheless, some churches have closed their Sunday Schools and given up the arduous business of running weeknight activities for young people. They have also abandoned the visiting of the community, and similar outreach activities, making the evangelism of holy living an excuse for being at ease in Zion.

Some kind of outline plan or policy is vital for every church, and it is clearly implied by the warfare analogy. Can we imagine a nation being at war without any plan or objectives? There are no end of matters that demand a great deal of thinking. If our location is poor for Sunday School work, perhaps we need to hire a school where the children live. We may be thankful to God we have a good building for the church, but if it is no good for the children, we will need to begin a branch. This is warfare thinking, but it is seldom seen today. There were numerous branches of churches and Sunday Schools years ago. Roland Hill at the old Surrey Chapel (a whole generation before Spurgeon) had thirteen branch Sunday Schools because he did not think much of the location and social image of the chapel for that purpose.

This is what the battle for souls is about. Fighting a war involves an entire army with its divisions, brigades and battalions, down to the companies and the platoons, and all have to be deployed in a co-ordinated way. This is like the labours in old-time authentic Calvinistic congregations. Does our church think in terms of reaching all levels of society, and using all the abilities of the membership in that task?

Another rather obvious observation about the warfare analogy of the New Testament is the enormous amount of *sacrificial activity* implied. War demands utmost commitment even in unreasonable conditions. If the command comes that a mission must be undertaken at midnight, the troops may not decline on the grounds that it is time to sleep. The military analogy points to inconvenience, difficulty and hardship. Is this the ethos in our churches, and the kind of situation we happily accept as individuals? A pastor was telling me that a plea for pianists for a weeknight children's meeting fell on deaf ears, despite the presence of many able pianists in that church. One after the other they declined because they had something else to do, or because their comfortable routine would be disturbed.

As a boy I once had an English master (actually a Welshman) who, at twenty-one, had been a junior officer in the First World War. He told of how he volunteered at the outbreak of war with twenty or so other young men who had been at university together. They had just started their careers, but felt they should serve their country, knowing it might mean loss of life or limb. There is a very famous documentary film clip of a boyish 2nd lieutenant nervously pacing to and fro in a trench, then waving his pistol and leading his men 'over the top', out of the trench. Such junior officers were so often the first to be cut down by enemy fire, and my English teacher was the only one among his friends to return from the war. They knew the risks, but they were ready to volunteer for king and country. Yet here are we today, children of the eternal King, called to a spiritual warfare, and yet so few will come forward to regular service in many churches. We have lost sight of the effort and injury of the war analogy, with all its sacrifice, cancelled home leave, and crawling about for days on frozen ground or in flooded trenches. The far more comfortable rigours of regular Christian service are unthinkable for so many reformed Christians.

I have known a number of people who had to move to a new location and a new church, where they observed there was no Sunday School. These were nice churches, with a good ministry and dear people who gave the new members warm encouragement when they wished to begin Sunday Schools. People said, 'What you are doing is wonderful and we are so grateful to you. We are with you in this.' And no doubt they were faithful in prayer, but (and this is a situation

I have heard from a number of people) no one ever lifted a finger to help in a practical way.

Just recently I met a couple who went from the Tabernacle to a provincial town nearly 25 years ago, and since then have faithfully operated a Sunday School in a sizeable reformed church of good reputation. But after all this time, when they go away on holiday, the School has to close because they have no helpers. What is wrong in our churches, whereby, when the Lord gives them a zealous couple who get down to work, they provide no challenge or training to others to join with them in the battle for souls? Is such spiritual indifference to the work of the Gospel authentic Calvinism? Of course not.

We should reflect the spirit of *Acts 20.16*, where the apostle Paul rushes to Jerusalem to take advantage of the Day of Pentecost, and the greatly swollen population of the city – people who could be reached with the Gospel. Where is the hunger for conversion today, apart from a desire for revival, when, it is hoped, God will do all the work for us?

Sometimes churches recoil from the battle because the enemy is considered to be unbeatable. Yet another military example occurs to us from World War II. How tragic it was when Britain lost Singapore in 1942! It was very difficult to defend Malaya, and so four British divisions retreated into Singapore, crossing the causeway and attempting to destroy it behind them. Eventually the Japanese invaded Singapore, taking the British by surprise by approaching from an unexpected direction. Within seven days General Percival had surrendered the British and Commonwealth forces, losing 9,000 in the battle, and sending into captivity 100,000 British and Commonwealth troops. Many authorities have called this the most humiliating defeat in the history of the British Army. In addition, 25,000 Chinese males between 18 and 60 were summarily executed by the Japanese. The British POWs went into abject slavery, most of them in Burma working on the railway.

Why did they surrender? It was because they thought the Japanese were far stronger than was the case. Afterwards it emerged that Japanese supplies were stretched to breaking point, so that they had only one or two weeks' fighting in them. But they were thought to be far stronger. Poor General Percival got the blame. He was by all accounts a gentleman, who had evidently wanted to follow Churchill's order to fight to the last drop of blood, but he proved weak before his fellow commanders and subordinated himself to their desire to surrender. It was all because they thought the enemy was unbeatable. Is this why we will not fight in the battle for souls today?

Do we look at the walls of atheism, and at the power of the media and the entertainment world, and retreat into our shells thinking the great commission can no longer be carried out? Accordingly the fight of faith today is fought in the arenas of truth, holiness, and the maintenance of assurance, but not in the battle for souls. May I say it again, that viewed in the light of our forebears reformed Christians today are a strangely lopsided entity. We are not like our forebears. We do not have the fervour or the urgency. We do not have the soul-winning priority. If only we would recognise this, we could begin to move forward once again. But the final word must be: what about ourselves as individuals? Do we see ourselves as those saved to serve? A true spirituality, a genuine personal spiritual life, means whole-hearted commitment or dedication to the Lord's service, and to the souls of lost men, women and children. The supreme task of our Lord and Saviour Jesus Christ, on earth, was to secure salvation. Ours is to make it known. This is our calling, our purpose, our joy, and our reward.

7
Everyone Has Special Gifts

A S WE ARE BONDSLAVES of Christ, it is obvious that our gifts must be dedicated to his service and employed in the church, and not entirely devoted to our earthly wellbeing. The progress of our spiritual life depends upon this. The truth that each believer has certain special gifts from the Lord is asserted in a number of Bible passages. 'Unto every one of us,' says Paul, 'is given grace according to the measure of the gift of Christ' *(Ephesians 4.7)*. He says that different gifts are distributed among us *(Romans 12.6; 1 Corinthians 12.6)*.

We are surely intended to recognise these gifts, and to employ them. 'As every man hath received the gift,' says Peter, 'even so minister the same one to another, as good stewards of the manifold grace of God' *(1 Peter 4.10)*. Paul says much the same in writing to Timothy – 'Neglect not the gift that is in thee' *(1 Timothy 4.14)*.

It is a great shame that when we speak of gifts we sometimes think only of sign-gifts, the miraculous gifts of the early church, and gifts to preach. The gifts of which Paul and Peter speak obviously go beyond these. They include 'natural' abilities (often increased and refined by God at the time of conversion), and also gifts of 'opportunity'. In one list of gifts Paul includes the gift of ruling, the ability to care for others, and the responsibility of large stewardship *(Romans 12.8)*.

This chapter will mention twenty-one possible gifts, although there are possibly more. It seems to this writer, but only on the basis of personal reflection, that every child of God probably has in some degree about a third of them. A few may possess more, but the interdependence of believers (suggested in such passages as *Ephesians 4.16* and *Colossians 2.19*) points to a somewhat even distribution of abilities. The Lord has probably put us all on the same footing, so that each believer has roughly the same number as another, and we therefore depend upon each other to make up a whole complement of abilities. This is a humbling as well as an uplifting probability. We are all significant, and must all exercise the gifts entrusted to us.

Before we list those special abilities, three brief points must be made. First, gifts are not given for our personal benefit, but for the advance of the church. When Paul mentions the gifts of apostles, prophets, evangelists, pastors and teachers, he says they were given, 'For the perfecting of the saints, for the work of the ministry, for the edifying of the body of Christ.' They were intended to bring churches to maturity, to 'the stature of the fulness of Christ' *(Ephesians 4.12-13)*. They were also given for the protection of the church: 'That we henceforth be no more children, tossed to and fro' *(Ephesians 4.14)*. This applies to all gifts or abilities given to believers. They are for the benefit of the church.

Secondly, the gifts of believers are to be employed in evangelism. Paul says: 'From whom *[Christ]* the whole body fitly joined together and compacted by that which every joint supplieth, according to the effectual working in the measure of every part, maketh increase of the body unto the edifying of itself in love' *(Ephesians 4.16)*. When all the gifts of members are employed, the church will grow.

Thirdly, most of these gifts are possessed by every Christian at least to some small degree. As we proceed through the following list, readers may think, 'Surely every Christian should do this.' An obvious example is the gift to witness. There is no doubt, however, that a *special* portion of each ability is distributed by God among believers, according to his will, and they should recognise this, and respond. We now list some of the gifts distributed around the people of God.

The first to be noted is the gift *to teach*. Every believer can teach to some extent. We teach our own children, and we explain things to one another. But there are some who possess a distinctive ability for this. They expound the Word, exhort the people and publicly reason with sinners to be saved. They, perhaps, can see the message in the Scripture more readily than others.

Yet this teaching gift is not restricted to preachers. Many have a great gift for teaching young people and children. Indeed, there are many good preachers who are no use at all for teaching children. One of the most noted preachers of the 20th century told of how he gave an address to children early in his ministry, and afterwards his wife told him he must never try it again. He complied, and never again spoke to children. The Lord has equipped many to reach children, who cannot teach adults.

This writer has known several people who have been remarkable teachers of children, so much so that they could quell and hold spellbound the most unruly gatherings. Yet he would never have imagined they possessed such power before seeing them in action. There are more gifted teachers than we sometimes realise, but they will never be apparent unless we watch for them. The Lord commanded all his people, saying, 'Pray ye therefore the Lord of the harvest, that he would send forth labourers into his harvest' (*Luke 10.2*). If we pray and watch, we might discover many capable people in our midst.

Another gift to be mentioned is that of *shepherding*. Sometimes shepherds are the least noticed people in a church fellowship, and yet they accomplish so much. This ability, like teaching, is often unexpected. There are people who are very retiring and unobtrusive, and you would never think of them as having a great influence upon others. Then you discover that they are among the most effective shepherds. They know how to engage and encourage others in a right and acceptable spirit. They have an eye for what is needed, and they possess the humility, gentleness and warmth to give vital help. Of course, all should possess this grace, but for some it is a special gift. They know how to advise, when to advise, and when not to advise. They know how to console, to comfort, to admonish, without a trace of hectoring or superiority. Some of the major troubles experienced in churches occur because people admonish others on sensitive issues when they have no real gift. In no time they set up shock-waves of reaction and offence. Shepherding is a great gift to the church. Perhaps the reader has such a gift. The possibility should not excite anyone to pride, after all, what is one gift among many? But if we recognise that we have a concern for others, and can see how they may be approached, and God gives us grace, then we have a responsibility to yield that gift to the service of the Lord.

The gifted shepherd is never a busybody, interfering in other people's lives in order to 'run' them. The true shepherd has the humility to know when a person should be referred to a pastor or elder. The gift is unobtrusively exercised, without drawing attention to the shepherd. This may well be the gift mentioned in *1 Corinthians 12.28 – helps*. But what kind of helps? They would be people of exceptional sensitivity and kindness, who possess the gift of friendship. They would have compassion for the fallen, sympathy for the troubled and great gentleness in the way they go about helping. Those helped would not see them as counsellors, but as friends. There is a special grace about them, and without them a fellowship is poor indeed.

Another highly valuable gift is the capacity for *discernment.* Every Christian has a measure of this, but some seem to have a most acute faculty. They may have a keen sense of danger, seeing problems long before others perceive them. It may be that a church is organising something, perhaps a children's activity, when a far-sighted member of the group will see a potential problem, or an omission, which must be taken account of.

There are cases where a person with a sense of spiritual danger would have saved a church from doctrinal disaster. Many years ago I knew a church that lost its minister, and another was to be called. The church became very attached to a young man who, however, was on an entirely different theological wavelength. Most of the members were too struck by his outgoing personality to notice his deficiencies, but there were one or two members who saw the danger very clearly, realising that this candidate possessed a woefully low view of Scripture, and a readiness to follow liberal and worldly trends.

One of these cautious brethren, an elderly, retired man who had served as a deacon, tried to bring the problem to the attention of the church leaders, but they would not listen. When the proposed appointment was discussed in a church meeting, this elderly brother expressed his concerns, but he was met with murmurs of impatience and disapproval. People did not want to listen. His fears were given no consideration. The young man was called as pastor, and the church eventually lost all depth of teaching and fell into the hands of the charismatic movement. One person saw the issues clearly, but his discernment was neither valued nor heeded. All the 'gifts' are important to a church, and people who see issues and their implications are precious. (When we speak of people gifted with special discernment, we do not of course mean those who are merely negative and critical about everything.)

Yet another gift is that of *organisation.* This extends beyond problem solving. There are people who can take up a proposed plan (not necessarily their own), and show how it can best be implemented. We need the gift of organisation to a special degree in church life because our workforce is composed almost entirely of volunteers, and this gives rise to numerous complications. It may be that a church operates a large Sunday School. Historically, churches have often had Sunday Schools as large as day-schools. We thank God for people who made it all work happily and harmoniously. Of course the organiser is dependent upon teachers and other workers for success, and should not be seen as a supremely special person, for that would give rise to great pride, and create a caste system in the church.

Yet another special ability, is that of *responsibility*. Every Christian should be responsible, but there are those who notice before anyone else that classes are falling in size, or that vital things are not being done, and they *feel* about it. Such people are the ones who are sure to turn out lights and lock doors. They are the most diligent at visiting their Sunday School children, and everyone recognises that they have 'a safe pair of hands'. They have the gift of responsibility and they cannot rest until their commitments are honoured. Responsibility is needed throughout the church, and it is certainly a prime qualification for office.

A notable gift is a special ability for *witness*. There are some who have better opportunities on account of where they work or who they mix with. They have access to many people, either at work or in college, and for them there may be a good openness to witness. While every believer must witness, for these people it is clearly *their* ministry. They possess an unusual capability. They are at ease in the work of witness. They enjoy ready acceptance with people and often have a natural fluency. They interact sympathetically and effectively, and seem unaffected by shyness. Anyone who has such a gift should not feel proud, but accountable. If God has bestowed such a gift it must be exercised, with prayer.

Another gift is that of *empathy*. Some Christians possess a strong natural relationship with certain categories of people. We have already referred to certain Sunday School teachers who, if we may put it like this, seem to have the power to cast a spell over children. They relate very naturally to them. Their gift cuts through all barriers, enabling them to control a class, however excitable. Others relate particularly well to the elderly; others with teenagers, so often on edge with those outside their peer group. The gift of empathy seems to equip possessors with an instinct for how to behave. They slip into a group as though they have known them for years and are accepted. Anyone who has received an ability for ease of association ought to be exercising it. How shall we face the Lord if such a gift has been allowed to lie dormant for years?

We now come to a gift which covers many talents. Virtually every believer has some *mental gift*, either with figures, or with languages, or with writing, and we should seek a way of exercising our mental capacity to the glory of God. In particular we shall comment here on the gift of *memory*. Some people have astonishing powers of recollection. They can remember names, faces, and circumstances of people in great detail. What a tragedy if that gift only fuels gossip and 'small talk'!

People sometimes talk to one another for hours about the affairs of others. Their remarkable memories are wasted, because they are not applied to the needs of other believers, or the progress of people under spiritual impressions. An excellent memory is a gift which is greatly refined by conversion. It is not for chitter-chatter and irrelevancies. Of course there has to be some 'small talk' in life, but the precious gift of recall is chiefly to be exercised in the work of God.

Another great gift is *imagination* or *vision* (but not having visions). Those equipped with this are seldom short of ideas for how teaching may be presented, or an impact made on the community. Bold visionaries are usually the first to see possibilities. If they head departments for the young they will always have something different in mind, in terms of special messages, themes or visual aids. Operating within the bounds of biblical orthodoxy, vision is a priceless gift of imagination. Unfortunately some possessors only exercise their gift at home. They decorate, then decorate again; they innovate and extend; but they never dream dreams about the work of the Lord. It would be much better for them to paint everything at home in one colour, and then apply their imagination to the work of the Lord.

Yet another valuable gift is that of *strong feeling*. How we value those who feel deeply about matters! They possess infectious enthusiasm and inject a welcome vigour and impetus into the work of God. They provide an example of strong emotional commitment, inspiring and motivating everyone with their warmth. When soul-searching and sorrow is called for, such people lead the way in this also. We are certainly glad everyone is not the same, because that would be overwhelming, but this gift can be one of the most important in the building of an active and sincere church.

This gift is balanced by another, the gift of *a cool brain*. After speaking with someone who possesses strong feelings, we sometimes find the cool-brained person a cold fish, but this is unfair. Such people may be as feelingful as anyone else, but it is locked inside them. They have a cautious mind and a reflective way of thinking. They are analytical, and often meticulous for detail. They are an anchor in the fellowship, giving stability, and acting as the cement that holds things together. They calm down enthusiasm when it runs to excess, not because they are negative people or 'wet blankets', but because they value realism. The one with strong feelings pours in enthusiasm, while the cooler person analyses and perfects matters. We need this blend of capacities and gifts.

Yet another gift is the *ability to work*. People so gifted have within them great energy and drive. This gift is different from enthusiasm, because the enthusiast may lead the field in emotional commitment, but may lack the strength to see a project through to the end, maintaining the effort. Some people are amazing workers. In some cases you wonder how their bodies can physically take it, because they are always on the go, seemingly having unlimited supplies of strength. What a blessing it is to have a scattering of people who have undying stamina. If you are gifted with this mental and physical discipline and application make sure it is applied to the Lord's work. Is it mainly directed outside the work of God, or is it directed within?

Some believers have *unusual strength for trial*. They are not just stoics, but they can stand up under great pressure. They can be patient in the most troubling circumstances. Whatever is hurled at them, or at the church, they will be sure to stand, and to show the rest of us how to stand also. They do not go to pieces. They are like extra buoyancy in a ship passing through turbulent seas. They have a gift combining patience, faith, courage and commitment to a high degree. Every fellowship needs those with such capacities as these.

A gift always appreciated among believers is the gift of *humour*. Humour goes hand-in-hand with the gift of *cheerfulness*, but they are different, because you can be cheerful without having a particularly productive sense of humour. Godly humour and cheerfulness lift people up, and help to keep difficult times sweet.

Some believers have the gift of *special faith in prayer*. I speak very carefully about this, because every child of God has the gift of prayer, but there is such a thing in Scripture as the gift of faith. Those who possess it have an unusually fruitful ministry of prayer. It is a calling, and they must exercise that gift.

Every believer also has the gift of *stewardship*, but there are some who have opportunities and provisions beyond the normal. God so guides them in life that they are prospered for this ministry. They are able to deploy their resources and substance to the glory of God in a large way. They have the power to maintain stewarding priorities, and God also gives them a humble mind, so that they do not use their wealth to buy influence, favours or reputation. 'He that giveth,' says the apostle, must do so 'with simplicity', that is, without any desire to be noticed and regarded for it, or to gain favour.

A similar gift is a special ability *to handle elevation in life*. We must all resist the temptations which come through success, but some people are especially strengthened to resist the pride, flattery, authority and self-pampering that comes with great promotion and prosperity. These are the people who God may place in positions of authority and privilege in society. They know how to contain and restrict themselves, and live with potentially dangerous advantages. They have the capacity to cope without being puffed up or becoming selfish.

Equally, there are those who have a powerful ability *to handle deprivation*, such as the apostle Paul. Pioneer missionaries especially need such a gift.

Some have the gift of *music*. I will not go into this to any extent, but ungifted believers envy those who are equipped with fine voices and excellent musical control. They are able to sing so well, but sometimes they do not exercise their gift. We are not talking about solos and choirs, but swelling the praise of God's people, and inspiring the young to sing. We are all accountable for what we do with our gifts and abilities.

There is also the gift of *producing beauty*. I am not referring to people who look beautiful, but those who seem to know what is beautiful. They know instinctively what colour to paint things, or how to arrange things. Possessors have a capacity to inject into Christian service, and into life in general, something rewarding to the human mind. They keep us off the rocks of ugliness and offensiveness. In our work for the Lord, even the laying out of literature, or of Sunday School displays, requires those who can work their arts to achieve good results.

There are many gifts or propensities, and we have suggested that no one has many more or less than anyone else, because the Lord has made us dependent upon each other as a mutually interdependent society. It is also worth reflecting that there may be gender evenness in the distribution of gifts. We must see the importance of our own gifts, and at the same time value the gifts of others. We should always keep in mind that gifts are presents, not being produced by our own ingenuity. We are responsible for how we employ them, and we must improve them by use. Pray for the use of whatever gifts you have. Remember above all that they are for the efficiency, enlargement and comfort of the Church of Jesus Christ.

It is a good thing to mark each decade of life with a review of what has been done with God-given aptitudes. When you pass out of your teens, you may have deep regrets for having neglected the exercise of your gifts. If you are in teenage you probably have greater opportunity to mix easily with other people than you will ever have in the future. Relating to people is easier. Resistance to the message of God may be less severe. You interact with peers before hardening of the heart makes them unapproachable. This is a precious time, and you may one day say, 'What did I do with those precious years?' Don't stroll through these years squandering these short-lived opportunities.

If you are in your twenties you have great energy, and the liberty to throw yourself into the corporate work of your church more than others. A spouse or children may not yet be part of your life. What will you have to show for your twenties?

Perhaps you now have a family, and are in your thirties. You have acquired more experience and new connections in your career. In your church, you may now have the scope to lead departments. Younger people respect you in a special way, because you are ahead of them, and yet near to them. What are you doing with your thirties? Are all your powers given to the work of God?

If you are in your forties, you are in a golden time of life. You now combine in your potential usefulness the best of everything. People respect you, your word can count, and your example will be followed. You are experienced and knowledgeable. You are in your early prime. In your fifties you will have more experience, but right now you combine knowledge with energy. You have many of an older person's attributes, united with a younger person's vitality. Will you one day look back in regret, because this priceless decade of your life passed in wasted years?

If you are in your fifties, your children may have grown up and do not need constant attention. This is very liberating. Now you have considerable experience, and being older, you can counsel and help others without appearing patronising. You may have greater substance for stewardship. Certainly, energy may begin to fade, and, for some, sicknesses be more frequent, but so much can still be done. Do not let the time go by, so that one day you will be harassed by vain regrets.

Value your abilities and opportunities. Praise God that he equips all his people to serve. Remain humble at all costs. Do not let the church of which you are a vital part limp along with your contribution missing. Let every man and woman employ their precious gifts all the way to glory. Without dedication of our gifts, how can we expect the blessing of communion with the Lord in the spiritual life?

8
Spiritual Encouragements
Pressures – Prayer – Encouragement – Thanksgiving

'Who comforteth us in all our tribulation, that we may be able to comfort them which are in any trouble, by the comfort wherewith we ourselves are comforted of God' *(2 Corinthians 1.4)*.

ONE OF THE BEST FEATURES of the spiritual life is the so-called 'cycle of grace', by which pressures move us to prayer, resulting in a great encouragement or blessing from God, leading to thanksgiving, followed so often by our using our blessing to bring help to other believers. Paul will say a good deal about 'comfort' from the fourth verse of *2 Corinthians 1*, but it is essential to know what he means by comfort.

The Greek word translated comfort is a very broad term, whereas 'comfort' has become a very narrow one. Who needs comfort? A child who is in pain, or an adult in grief. Comfort soothes; whether it is the doctrinal comfort we derive from the Bible, or whether simple friendship. But when Paul speaks of comfort, as the passage will show, he refers mainly to *encouragement.* According to the way we use words today, comfort eases, whereas encouragement spurs and strengthens. Consolation is certainly included in Paul's language, but most of all, encouragement. Every time we read of comfort in this passage, *encouragement* is the golden ingredient to remember.

Speaking about himself and Timothy, Paul testifies to God's comfort 'in all our tribulation'. *Tribulations* are literally pressures. But how can we be sure that comfort here means *encouragement*? Paul tells us (in verse 5) that these troubles are 'the sufferings of Christ' that abound in us. From this we learn what he is talking about, because the pressures that were upon Christ were opposition, enmity and persecution, and these were also the pressures upon Paul and his fellow preachers. Their tribulations, troubles and sufferings in this passage are chiefly those things which came because of their work for Christ.

The Lord, however, saw them through by giving them great *encouragements* in answer to their prayers. He intervened in their difficulties, delivered them, and provided for them, and Paul wants the Corinthians to experience the same blessings. He wants them to look for similar encouragements in their evangelistic difficulties. Of course it is true that God will comfort us with divine sympathy and assurance in all kinds of trouble, and we will speak of these comforts to other believers so that they in turn look to God for help. But the primary application of these verses is to Christian workers experiencing trouble or resistance, even perhaps painful persecution like that of the apostle.

The non-violent antagonism that we have in our land today will similarly be balanced, in answer to prayer, by many deliverances, provisions and triumphs of grace. We would love to be able to knock the doors with the result that the people came readily out to the services. Equally we would love to be able to speak through the public media, and to challenge the atheism of the day, but there are pressures against us. We are shut out, pushed back, belittled and scorned. This may be so, says the apostle to us, but I want to tell you how the Lord has encouraged us, because he will similarly encourage you. This is the meaning of his words – 'who comforteth us *[encourages us]* . . . that we may be able to comfort them which are in any trouble, by the comfort wherewith we ourselves are comforted of God.'

Remarkably, Paul goes further, saying that the encouragement will be commensurate with the tribulations. Note his words – 'For as the sufferings of Christ abound in us, so our consolation *[encouragement]* also aboundeth by Christ.' For every pressure against us for Christ's sake, there will be an encouragement to help us, and this is one of God's marvellous promises to his witnessing people. What are the encouragements? Clearly, answered prayer and Gospel success, together with inner assurance, deliverances and provisions. When the lost are won to Christ, and rebels return, we have all the comfort or encouragement we could desire to balance the pressures and the difficulties.

Consider the *scale* of the encouragements implicit in Paul's words: 'For as the sufferings of Christ *abound* in us, so our consolation also *aboundeth* by Christ.' These 'abounding' words are strong words in the Greek. If the pressures are numerous and heavy, so the encouragements will super-abound as we serve the Lord.

So what are these encouragements? An example will be given by Paul (from verse 8), but, as we have noted, they are deliverances, experiences of strength and assurance, great provisions, and, of course, spiritual fruit, all in answer to prayer. Paul is teaching a golden chain of blessing – pressures, prayer, encouragement, thanksgiving. We accept the pressures and the sufferings, turn to the Lord in prayer, consequently receive the encouragement, and then give thanks and praise to God. Paul passed this procedure to his converts, and they in turn passed it on, and we are still proving it today.

Let me give an example of this from around 1959. I was twenty at the time, engaged in National Service, and in London on leave for a few days. I went to a missionary meeting held by a church that gave support to two wonderful ladies who only seven years previously had set up the Christian hospital and mission known as 'the Shining Hospital' in Pokhara, Nepal. I dare say many readers know the remarkable story.

The speaker at the meeting was Dr Lily O'Hanlon who with Miss Hilda Steele had founded the hospital. Of course by this time they were middle-aged, but they had met in the 1930s soon after Dr O'Hanlon qualified in medicine, Hilda having just trained for missionary service. They both felt very strongly that there ought to be a mission hospital in this particular part of Nepal. There were other hospitals in the land, but no Christian mission or hospital, and the government of the time did its utmost to clamp down on Christianity, keeping out all Westerners, apart from ambassadors and other special people. These ladies tried hard to get into Nepal for sixteen years, labouring for the Lord in North India, praying and hoping that one day they would be able to cross the border.

After World War II, their hopes rose when the British ambassador in Kathmandu invited them to have a holiday with him, with an eye to securing admission for them. Hopes were raised only to be dashed, and this happened several times over as permission was given only to be rescinded. But the ladies prayed on, until eventually in 1952 they were allowed to enter.

They trekked on foot all the way to Pokhara to begin their longed-for labour for the Lord. It became one of those glorious missionary stories of how the Lord remarkably provided building materials for the project, notably the roofing for the buildings. Unexpectedly, local people knew about metal sheets buried in wartime by the British army to prevent them falling into the wrong hands. The ground was duly dug, and these corrugated aluminium or galvanised iron sheets were recovered, soon forming the gleaming roofs, which led to the well-known name, the Shining Hospital.

Yet another of countless testimonies to the overruling of God passed into the annals of the Christian church, recording how pressures (when all doors were shut, and everything seemed impossible) led to prayer, and this led in God's time to mighty encouragement and thanksgiving. This was the story I heard from the intrepid missionary doctor in 1959, and this is how it affected me (along with similar testimonies) three or four years later, when my wife and I were pioneering a church in Borehamwood, north of London. We needed a site, and we had a similar problem. The London County Council owned everything. They had bought every square inch of land in that Hertfordshire district to build Borehamwood as a London overspill town, and they were adamant that there would be no land for a pioneer church. The door was slammed shut.

Now for ourselves, I freely admit, we would have said, 'Well, that's that! Officialdom has ruled that it cannot be done.' Yet we tried again, and again. What made us persist? What made us continue to knock on that firmly closed door, and to pray for change? The answer is, we had our heads full of shining hospitals. We had heard so many accounts of great encouragements experienced by Christians under pressure, all the way down from the apostle Paul. We were so deeply influenced by this powerful tradition of proving the Lord (pressures, prayer, encouragement, and thanksgiving) that we followed the same policy.

We were not naturally insistent people, or characterised by unrealistic expectations. We were not filled with overwhelming self-confidence, thinking we could take on the then mighty London County Council. But we were trained by all that we had heard to believe that the Lord is all-powerful. As events unfolded, by remarkable overruling, circumstances dramatically changed, and in due course a very large site, and then a building were secured.

Look again at the words of Paul (verse 4), speaking of God – 'who comforteth [encourages] us in all our tribulation [pressures], that we may be able to comfort them which are in any trouble, by the comfort wherewith we ourselves are comforted of God.' As soon as we see that 'comfort' applies not only to our personal griefs, but more directly to the encouragements that come to us in the Lord's service, then we understand that Paul is saying that he passes on the principle to other labourers for Christ – pressures, prayer, encouragement, thanksgiving.

I am sometimes concerned about fine young Christians in the Tabernacle on this matter. If the Lord saves you in a large church, where the bills all seem to be paid, and everything seems to be accomplished by willing hands, it could happen that you miss out on proving the Lord by this recurring cycle of pressures, prayer, encouragement and thanksgiving. You may need to be inspired and stimulated by the apostle's experience and by the numerous accounts of answered prayer from the annals of Christian blessing.

Once these are in your heart, you have this often repeated experience yourselves. You witness, and get no hearing. You join in the contact or visitation work, and nothing happens. You staff the Saturday market bookstall, but no one comes to church as a result. You knock the doors in the community only to be rebuffed. Then you realise that personal charm, fluency or persuasiveness cannot accomplish anything. You find everyone against you in your place of work or study, and you feel really isolated, rejected and under pressure.

But now you remember Paul and all his troubles, and how, by prayer and trust, he was able to turn the Gentile world upside down. You remember also shining hospitals of many kinds in the records of missionary endeavour, and then you call on the Lord with all your heart. Inevitably, in due time, blessing, provision and victory comes. This is 'pressures, prayer, encouragement, thanksgiving' in action, and how much we must learn it, prove it and hold to it. This is a life of faith, and the Lord will build that faith in our hearts by this procedure.

Be great readers, especially of reformers and pioneer missionaries, and be inspired by the policy of faith. We never say, 'I can do nothing, therefore I will do nothing,' expecting the Lord to bring people into the kingdom by entirely miraculous means. We willingly accept our labour for him, but we carry it out with a profound sense of inability and emptiness, accepting that circumstances will heap themselves against us. But encouragements will eventually be given, and our hearts will rejoice before the Lord. We have this treasure, Paul will shortly say, in earthen vessels, that is in simple, useless pots, so that the power may be clearly seen to be God's and not ours.

The apostle gives a harrowing example of a near-fatal trial suffered by himself and Timothy shortly before writing *2 Corinthians*. The terrible tribulation led to prayer, and from prayer came a spectacular deliverance, leading to thanksgiving. He then asks the Corinthians to pray with him for future deliverances in the service of Christ, the cycle of faith appearing clearly in his words: 'Ye also helping together by prayer for us, that for the gift bestowed upon us *[of deliverance]* by the means of many persons *[praying]* thanks may be given by many on our behalf' *(2 Corinthians 1.11)*.

We must never allow the devil to lull us into a sense of comfort, isolated from all concerns, because the congregation is large and the bills seem to be paid smoothly. We must share in every pressure that comes upon a Gospel-proclaiming congregation. We must feel along with others our corporate inadequacy and need, calling upon the Lord, experiencing his mighty provisions, and then swelling the praise and thanksgiving due to his name. This process is an ever-recurring cycle of wonder and adventure in the lives of the servants of Jesus Christ. This is the perpetual motion of the spiritual life; a golden chain, a cycle of grace.

9
The Power of Prayer
Do You Have a Ministry of Intercession?

'I exhort therefore, that, first of all, supplications, prayers, intercessions, and giving of thanks, be made for all men' *(1 Timothy 2.1).*

I T IS OFTEN SAID that a priest is one who represents God to man, and who also represents man before God. Christian believers are the 'priests' of the church age; in fact, in the Bible we are described as a kingdom of priests. In our witness we speak from God to man, carrying out the first function of a priest, and in pleading in prayer to God for people we carry out the second. Do we as individual believers exercise such a ministry of intercession?

The exhortation of *1 Timothy 2.1* speaks of making representation for all men, and this definitely includes those who are unconverted, because Paul goes on to say that God desires the salvation of lost souls (verse 4). Elsewhere Paul exhorts that prayer and supplication be made for 'all saints' also *(Ephesians 6.18).* There falls to each one a very remarkable privilege, because the God who commands intercession is undoubtedly the God who is moved by intercession, and ready to be prevailed upon, in the mystery of his will. It is very probable that every believer who reads these words was the subject of someone's earnest intercession prior to their conversion. Who prayed for us? We may know, or we may not know, but in all likelihood someone was pleading for us. Do we now plead for others?

It is not difficult to see some of the reasons why the ministry of intercession should have been given to us by the Lord. First, it produces largeness of heart in the interceder, so that we care much more for others, and for their souls. What a difference this ministry makes to the character of a believer who takes it seriously. That which occupies our prayer time occupies the very soul, and shapes our values.

Secondly, it fixes firmly in the heart the mission of Christ as the highest priority in the Christian's life. This becomes our theme above all others when we are consistent interceders.

Thirdly, the ministry of intercession brings us nearer to Christ in likeness and habit, for he, as our Great High Priest, is the eternal Interceder. As he prayed for us *(John 17)*, so we pray for others.

Fourthly (extending our first point), the ministry of intercession helps to make believers outgoing and unselfish. These virtues are stirred up by prayer, and then spread through our life.

Fifthly, this is a ministry unlike all others, because it is for every kind of Christian in every kind of situation. It is a ministry for the healthy, and also a ministry for the infirm. Intercession from the sick-bed may, for all we know, be more used by God than the act of preaching to thousands.

Sixthly – and this is of immense significance – intercession firmly establishes in our hearts that all praise and glory is due to God alone. As we pray, so the lost are delivered, and as we pray, believers are blessed. When, on the other hand, we witness without intercession, nothing ever seems to come of it. The constant interceder is persuaded from experience that *all* the glory is the Lord's.

The *scope* of the ministry of intercession extends beyond the following themes, but these represent most of our concerns and desires:–

- The conversion of lost individuals
- The preservation and protection of the Lord's people ('Pray one for another,' says James)
- The growth and peace of Christians
- The instrumentality of Christians
- The healing of others
- The keeping of the young from the world
- The blessing of Gospel workers

The first major example of intercessory prayer in the Bible is that of Abraham pleading for the life of Lot and his household (recorded in *Genesis 18*). The passage in which Abraham 'bargains' with God is so well known that we will simply make a few observations without attempting to describe the whole event. When the Lord said he would inspect Sodom, Abraham knew at once that it would be destroyed for its great evil. Immediately he 'stood yet before the Lord' *(Genesis 18.22)*, showing his firm purpose. Abraham's intercession would not be made merely out of a sense of duty, or lightly, but his mind would be totally engaged, and his heart wholly involved. He obviously believed that his pleading might prevail with the Lord, and so must we.

Abraham asks for the sparing of Sodom if fifty righteous souls are found there, appealing to the justice of God. Nevertheless, he is sure that 'the Judge of all the earth' will do what is right, and he assents to God's sovereign and perfect will. We also plead to prevail, but not to dictate to the Lord. Abraham's language is especially significant when he says, 'Behold now, I have taken upon me to speak unto the Lord, which am but dust and ashes.' He also says a little later, 'Oh let not the Lord be angry, and I will speak yet but this once.' The great patriarch knew that only *humble* intercession is acceptable with God, and we also must see this to plead successfully.

Abraham employs a technique to humble himself, in this case, classifying himself as mere dust and ashes, and we also should find ways of preparing our hearts in humility. We may reflect on our unworthiness, foolish deeds, sins of omission and commission, long trying of the Lord's patience and other aspects of our inadequacy before God, so that we come before him without pride or merit, and truly esteem him, and submit to him as we plead. We note that Abraham's pleadings were heard and answered, but not in the way he expected. The city was destroyed, but Lot was saved out of it, a far wiser solution than that proposed by Abraham. The essence of his prayer was rewarded, though not the detail. So it is with us today, as the Lord frequently answers in an ultimately far better way than that posed in our prayers.

The pleading of Moses

Moses also was a remarkable interceder, pleading repeatedly for the people even when they were hostile toward him. When God proposed the destruction of the people *(Exodus 32.9ff)*, Moses cried out most passionately, pleading for the preservation of the good name and glory of the Lord in the eyes of the Egyptians, and also pleading the promises of God made to the patriarchs. The verses recording his prayer must be noted as an example of acceptable prayer *(Exodus 32.11-13)*, for the Lord heard it, and Israel was preserved. Intercession is always feelingful. It is to be carried on despite aggravation from those for whom we pray, and it must long for the honour and glory of God in souls spared.

In the same 32nd chapter of *Exodus* we see Moses is so concerned for the people that he asks to be blotted out of the book of God if it would avail for their deliverance. Astonishingly, this plea follows their wickedness in making the golden calf. In this prayer Moses fulfils his role as a type of Christ, who substituted his life for his people. In the case of Moses, the offer was not acceptable with God, but the strong feeling behind it, even though the people had made themselves odious to him, shows how conscientiously he took his 'priestly' office and responsibility as an intercessor. If only we could accept the same level of responsibility for those among whom the Lord has set us!

Samuel's unwavering prayers

In some ways the most notable intercessor of all was Samuel, the prophet born through prayer, whose name means – 'Asked for of God'. In *1 Samuel 12.23*, he speaks to the people his famous words, 'God forbid that *I should sin against the Lord* in ceasing to pray for you.' To cease to intercede is a sin! It is a repudiation of our priesthood. It is a grotesque sin of ingratitude to God for all his grace, and to those who once prayed for us. It is a crime of great hardness and indifference to others. Do we sin in this way?

Like Moses, even though aggravated, Samuel would pray, forcefully expressing his determination never to stop. He says, 'God forbid that I should sin against the Lord *in ceasing* to pray for you.' It was his calling and office to intercede, just as it is ours today. We note that he would not *cease* to pray, showing that it was his regular habit to intercede. For us also there should be *daily* intercession especially for members of our family, for work colleagues, for members of our church, and for the Lord's servants. If the list of people grows too long, we may need to apportion it across the week, because we should never fall to merely naming names, with perhaps only a sentence for each one, but always plead with some measure of detail.

The people knew well that Samuel interceded for them, and when under fear or conviction they pressed him to do so *(1 Samuel 12.19)*. It is nothing to be ashamed of if people should know that we pray for them – saved or unsaved. Ultimately, it secures all the glory for God. It was Samuel who said to a sinful and oppressed people – 'I will pray for you unto the Lord.' The result was – 'And Samuel cried unto the Lord for Israel; and the Lord heard him' *(1 Samuel 7.5 and 9)*. We should not overlook the fact that the word 'cried' conveys great earnestness and desire.

Samuel is famous in the Bible as an intercessor. In *Psalm 99* we read of 'Moses and Aaron among his priests, and *Samuel* among them that call upon his name; they called upon the Lord, and he answered them.' When the Lord rejects the Jews through the lips of Jeremiah, he says: 'Though Moses and Samuel stood before me, yet my mind could not be toward this people.' What an astounding proof this divine statement is about the *normal* effectiveness of their earnest intercession. Even Moses and Samuel – usually persuasive and successful in their pleading – could not prevail once the Lord's patience was withdrawn.

Advice for interceders

Here are a number of items of advice for intercession drawn from the way our Old Testament forebears and examples went about it.

We should pray for more than names, asking *for specific blessings.* Vague intercession is not true intercession. Let us take each name separately and ask for a distinctive benefit.

We should *feel* for those for whom we pray, contemplating, for example, their terrors if eternally lost, or their pain if sick.

We should *labour* to represent them, as if we truly desired to persuade the Lord. How easily earnestness drains from private prayer! It may be an act of toil to maintain it.

We should pray *persistently* and *regularly*, never relaxing until the Lord answers from on high (or until the sin unto death is very clearly seen to have been committed).

We should be careful to *esteem believers* when we pray for them, so that our intercession does not become a superior or condescending act, as though we were praying for needy inferiors. The fallen heart is so subtle, and prayer should never be contaminated by a patronising or proud spirit.

We should pray much for our Sunday School class, or whoever else we have special responsibility for. The praying teacher becomes inevitably a visiting teacher, because he or she cares.

We should always give time to pray for *Christian workers*, both ministers and others.

We should be aware of the *trials* of workers and their *special opportunities*, bringing all as specific matters before the Lord, and we should not forget to give thanks over resulting blessing.

Occasionally it is helpful in the time of prayer to make intercession even before repenting of sin, for it engages the soul and draws the praying believer away from self. But if possible, heartfelt repentance should precede intercession, for it is the prayer of the righteous person, the cleansed person, which avails much. Once again, the need to pray with *fervour* and *desire* must be emphasised, because we surely will not be heard praying for things we do not care about. We also need a sense of audience, an atmosphere of awe, and an attitude of humility.

We believe that if all the members of a church were to engage in intercessory prayer, the outcome would be blessing on a wonderful scale. It is well known that the American 1858 revival began with the widespread take-up of intercession for individuals. By intercessory prayer we shall become instrumental, mightily encouraged, great blessing will come, and God will receive the glory.

The personal spiritual life of a 'priest' of God cannot advance if there is no priestly function of intercession. If our intercessions are few and small, we must take up this vital and privileged duty at once. Make a list, prepare the heart, and stand before the Lord. In even ten minutes we can intercede for many; but keep it up every day. And however you pray, or however long, remember that a measure of detail, specific praying, real desire, and fervour are all part of the Christian's priestly intercessory work.

For more help on the prayer life, see *The Lord's Pattern for Prayer*, Wakeman Trust, from which this chapter is taken.

10
Sincerity First and Foremost
in the Christian Armour of Ephesians 6.14

O F ALL THE CHRISTIAN VIRTUES, love is named in the
New Testament as the greatest and first *(1 Corinthians 13;
Galatians 5)*, but when several virtues are presented as the
Christian's armour, *sincerity* is the piece which must be donned first
as foundational to all others. If not the 'greatest' it is an essential
virtue on which other virtues depend. Do we possess it? And do we
know how to maintain it?

Paul speaks of putting on the whole armour of God in order to
resist the wiles or strategies of the devil. The 'whole armour' refers to
the full range of armour and weapons, not just the protective suit of
metal. Both offensive and defensive weapons are included. The need
for armour is because evil spirits of terrifying power and cunning
employ their strategies against us, including temptations to sin and
the undermining of assurance. In addition the demons of darkness

constantly strive to distract us from our mission for souls, seeking to bring down all witness if they can. They may do this by dangling in front of us worldly attractions, and shaking our priorities, so that God's work is no longer our chief aim. They want to bring individuals and churches to spiritual coldness and lethargy. They also assail with 'doctrines of demons', introducing into sound churches false ideas and false methods. How much we need the armour of God!

Paul tells us to take the whole armour of God – 'that ye may be able to withstand in the evil day'. What is the evil day? To some extent every day is an evil day because the devil never sleeps. But there are some days and some seasons when Satan and his host are particularly ferocious. Sometimes they call off their assault in order to bring us to a false sense of security, but then suddenly they try multiple temptations together. But the armour of God is sufficient, if only we employ it. Paul's words – 'Stand therefore' – are full of determination, and as individual believers and as churches we must respond – 'We will give no ground.'

We must stand firm in all attempts to draw us either into sin or away from the great mission of Christ. We must resist all the assaults of heresies, false methods and irreverent worship, with great determination. But how do we get such determination? The answer lies in the first piece of armour. 'Stand therefore,' says the apostle, 'having your loins girt about with *truth*.'

To see the full significance of this belt of truth we must briefly describe the armour of a Roman soldier. He had a sword, and possibly a short sword also, more like a very large knife. He was usually sent out with two javelins, and to defend himself he had a shield. His clothing consisted of a broad belt, thought to be six to eight inches wide, even larger than a present-day weight-lifting belt, made of leather a quarter of an inch thick or more. This was covered by vertical strips of iron, so that the belt was flexible, yet provided protective metal over the midriff. From this belt a kind of leather skirt extended, also covered with strips of metal to protect the thighs.

On his legs the soldier wore greaves, an old word for what we would call shin-pads, only larger, made of metal, and strapped on firmly. Then he had a helmet and a breastplate.

Foundational to all was the belt, not only because it provided protection but because the breastplate and backplate were donned rather like a sandwich board, then anchored to the belt, front and back. The sword and knife were also holstered to the belt, together with the javelins – attached by clasps. It is thought that even the shield was attached to the backplate and belt, with other articles also. The belt, therefore, was the firm foundation for other components. In addition it 'braced' the soldier ready for action.

With all this in mind, the apostle lists the items vital for Christian warfare, beginning with the words – 'having your loins girt about with truth'. Naturally we want to know what is meant here by truth. Does the apostle mean – 'before you put on any other item of spiritual armour, put on the Truth, or the fundamental doctrines of the faith'? This interpretation would certainly make sense, but it cannot be correct because doctrinal truth is mentioned later as – 'the sword of the Spirit, which is the word of God'.

Perhaps, then, 'truth' in this passage means that we must put on first and foremost *honesty*. This, too, is unlikely as honesty (a basic moral value) is surely included in 'the breastplate of righteousness', mentioned later. So what is meant by having one's loins girt about with truth? The best interpretation is that it means truthfulness in the sense of sincerity and genuineness. Says Paul, put around your loins the girdle, the belt, of sincerity, which will firmly hold all the other Christian virtues vital to your spiritual warfare.

Sincerity is a priceless virtue, given as a gift by the Spirit at conversion. This is implied in the illustration of the armour of the Roman soldier, because this was not manufactured or purchased by the soldier but provided for him. He simply collected his equipment from the armoury, and so it is with sincerity. It is a gift. We cannot create sincerity within us; it must be given to us by the power of

God. The heart is deceitful above all things, and the belt of genuineness, guilelessness and sincerity must come from God alone.

There has never been a true convert who was not made deeply sincere. Sadly, much of this 'birth' sincerity can slip away, but God will restore, renew and strengthen it on application. We have all known people who were proud, unteachable, devious, subtle and self-seeking before conversion, but one of the great signs of God's regenerating work was the arrival of real sincerity, and this must continue to be the foundation for everything else.

The belt of sincerity is powerful *defensive* armour, because it makes it much more difficult for the devil to bring us down. A sincere believer is conscientious about conduct, recoiling from duplicity, hypocrisy, and anything else which would undermine the work of the Lord.

However, the belt of sincerity may also be viewed as an *offensive* weapon, for it held the soldier's swords and spears. It is productive for the Gospel because unsaved people will usually respect and listen to people who are very evidently sincere. All but the most hardened people respect sincerity. Like the soldier's belt, sincerity also braces and nerves believers for battle, moving us to do the best we can for the Lord, and to prepare ourselves personally and prayerfully for spiritual endeavour. It is insincerity which is confident and casual about matters.

There are several words for sincerity in the Greek New Testament, one meaning – tested by the sun and found to be pure and genuine. Another means 'legitimate' or legitimately born, pointing away from pretence and hypocrisy. Still another Greek word translated 'sincere' means without decay, free from rot. In other words, a sincere person is utterly genuine and consistent. The devil hates sincerity, because he was a liar from the beginning. Sincerity repels him and makes him loath to come near to us. By contrast, insincerity encourages satanic attack. 'A double minded man,' says James, 'is unstable in all his ways.'

Insincerity accommodates an alternative agenda in the mind, so that we partly intend to pursue Christian aims, but worldly ideas, delights and ambitions also clamour for attention in our mind. The sincere person has only one objective, which is to please and serve the Lord, and this constitutes a built-in protection against Satan and backsliding. Sincerity, as the foundational belt for other virtues, makes our zeal pure.

Zeal without sincerity is sometimes produced by a desire to be seen doing things for the Lord. Sincerity, however, purifies our motives, so that we want to see souls saved and Christ alone glorified. Sincerity makes us averse to sin and inclined to obey the Lord. Sincerity is always conscientious, the sincere person keeping his promises whether made to the Lord, to the church, or to society in general, and keeping up his duties and responsibilities.

A sincere person finds boasting distasteful to him. He cannot put on a front, or dishonestly exaggerate his accomplishments.

A sincere person is far less likely to be ill-natured or ill-tempered, because in such moods we usually see things in an exaggerated or false way, and sincerity cannot do this. Sincerity, therefore, is a great protection; a foundation item in the armour of sanctification. Without the girdle of sincerity, the breastplate of righteousness cannot be properly attached. Paul concludes the 'Christian armour' passage with a powerful call to prayer, but there is little prayer when there is little sincerity, and without prayer the rest of the armour is useless.

How does pre-conversion insincerity return to the life of the believer? It creeps in under a number of circumstances, the first being double-mindedness, referred to earlier. We may want blessing for the church and for souls, and we may want to know more of Christ, but if we put alongside these godly desires selfish and worldly aims, so that we have dual objectives, we forfeit sincerity. To extend the apostle's military illustration, we take our place on the Lord's side, but also have interests on the other side. What kind of a soldier will such a person make? What level of zeal can we have if we have sympathies for godless aspects of this present world?

Deviousness also jettisons sincerity. If, for example, we hide things in our lives that we would not want other Christians to know about, becoming secretive and unstraightforward, how can sincerity survive? Lying certainly shatters sincerity.

Another sure way of undermining sincerity is to allow our sense of the danger, strength and power of the enemy to be diminished. Sincerity depends on reality. It has a serious quality and cannot co-exist with shallow overconfidence. It deeply desires to stand in the spiritual battle, and cannot survive in a person who makes no effort to keep in view the weakness of the heart and the great cunning of Satan.

Sincerity will certainly fade away if as Christians we no longer want to win the battle for souls and for holiness. If, for example, we don't particularly want to witness, and opt out of Christ's mission, we are bound to suppress our sincerity, because we once gave ourselves wholly and unreservedly to the Lord, and have gone back on our vows. We have probably repeated our first pledge to Christ many times, reconsecrating ourselves and yielding ourselves afresh, but we no longer intend to keep all these promises. Where is sincerity then? Similarly if we no longer hunger and thirst for righteousness, we have abandoned our promises, have cheated the Lord, and lost our integrity.

Sincerity also evaporates once we lose our realisation that the Lord's eye is upon his people all the time. The awareness that we are in the Lord's view constantly is the bulwark and bedrock of sincerity. With this knowledge we cannot take licence to do anything we like, and we react properly to all the trials of life. Christ is near and knows all, and this consciousness is the fire and life of true sincerity.

So sincerity is broken by divided allegiance, by double-living, by the omission of Christian duties, by loss of our sense of danger, by our no longer wanting to fight and win the good fight of faith, and by insensitivity to the watchful presence of the Lord. Sincerity – that vital gift from the Lord – is ripped from us by all these things, giving way to hardness of heart and ultimately to the cancer of hypocrisy. When we consider these pitfalls, we are only too glad sincerity may be reactivated by repentance before God, rededication, and the earnest renewing of our vows.

It is one thing to know what puts sincerity at risk, but how do we positively put it on as a Roman soldier would buckle on his belt? Firstly and obviously, we pray for it. We pray for all kinds of things but do we pray with great desire for sincerity? We can strengthen our desire for it if we see the ugliness and the weakness of insincerity. To be horrified by insincerity urges us to watch our hearts and to pray for the opposite. Constantly we need to ask ourselves, 'Am I real? Am I genuine? Am I truly sincere in my faith and in my walk?' Such thoughts and challenges will drive us to pray for sincerity.

Another great spur to putting on sincerity is to think of the cost of the soul purchased by Christ on Calvary's cross. Reflect on what he has spent on us, and what he has done for us. He did not suffer immeasurable agonies in body and soul to purchase phoney, half-committed, spiritually anaemic, reluctant, compromised, vacillating Christians. Do we not want to be made in *his* image?

To put on the belt of sincerity we must be determined to respond to the movement of conscience whenever it troubles us by the spurring of the Holy Spirit. When drawn by some sinful desire, or inclined to a wrong mood or reaction, or some white lie or spiteful word comes to our lips, will we be ready and willing to heed the warning voice of conscience? Will we respond, and immediately put an end to the rising sin? Responsiveness to conscience, and eagerness to promptly obey, is a large part of 'putting on sincerity'. But to suppress conscience, even for a moment, is to throw off the belt of sincerity.

To put on the belt of sincerity we determine to be very specific in our praying. By contrast, to generalise with God in prayer is to foster insincerity. For example, when it comes to prayer time, we should not repent superficially, merely praying, 'Lord forgive me, I repent.' This cannot be sincere repentance, but only foolish, shallow self-delusion. We must remember what we have done, or at least the broad pattern of sins on our conscience, for which we need forgiveness. We must name them, and feel the burden and shame of them, and pledge a better course of action to avoid them. Shallow or generalised repentance is counterfeit repentance, inconsistent with sincerity.

Similarly, as we noted earlier, in prayers of intercession, specific people should be on our mind and heart, who should be interceded for with compassion and desire. General sentiments are empty, easy, lazy, and insincere. Preachers often quote these well-known lines to illustrate this kind of superficiality:

> *I knelt in prayer when day was done,*
> *And prayed, 'O God, bless everyone.'*

Of course, public prayer cannot always be so specific, but in private prayer, 'God bless the persecuted!' is not enough. By being more specific in all our prayers we fasten firmly around us the girdle of sincerity.

To put on sincerity we must seek to be consistent people, keeping spiritual priorities uppermost even when we are exceptionally busy and responsibilities press upon us. We must put on the belt of sincerity in every department of life, family life, personal life and business life, never allowing spiritual goals and prayer to be washed away.

Sincerity is outstandingly beautiful, enhancing and adorning the personality and character of every kind of person. From the very simplest believer to the greatest intellectual, sincerity makes everyone far more attractive. The oldest believer is enriched and elevated by it, and so is the youngest. As we have noted, it is respected by all unsaved onlookers, commending the believer and his message more than almost anything else, particularly to the young. One of the remarkable features of children is that they unerringly discern sincerity or insincerity. (It is curious that such perception seldom survives beyond childhood.) If we are sincere people, our Sunday School children will listen to us, and our own children will respect us.

However, the greatest of all the benefits flowing from sincerity is that Christ will come in to us by his Spirit, to give greater light and blessing. Insincerity, like pride, drives him away.

The *father* of sincerity is gratitude, and if we keep alive and active a feelingful gratitude to God for all that he has done for us, sincerity will be greatly strengthened. The *mother* of sincerity is love, so that if we love the Lord with all our heart, this will help increase our sincerity. The *brother* of sincerity is faith, for the one always strengthens the other. The *sister* of sincerity is diligence, and if we are diligent and conscientious, especially in spiritual matters, we will maintain sincerity.

So let us say: 'Lord, make me and keep me sincere and genuine in my spiritual life, my family life, and my behaviour in the world.' Put on the girdle of truth, or sincerity! What protection it provides! What strength lies in this! And what an example is laid down for others!

Sincerity is the basis of our determination to please God and to defeat the devil. It makes us faithful and loyal in whatever we have undertaken, enables us to stand, and is a jewel in the personality and character of the possessor. Sincerity in its members will protect the church from the powers and rulers of the darkness of this world, and make it diligent and effective in the defence of the Truth. Sincerity will spur us to fulfil the great commission of the Lord. Precious, humble, radiant sincerity or genuineness is undoubtedly what is laid before us in *Ephesians 6.14*: 'Stand therefore, having your loins girt about with truth.'

11
Humility Essential for Blessing
'Serving the Lord with all humility of mind' (Acts 20.19).

THESE WORDS ARE FROM the parting speech of Paul to the Ephesian church elders, when they met with him at Miletus. They knew him well as he had been the founder of their church and its pastor for three years. How they loved him, especially for his total dedication to the work of Christ and to their spiritual welfare. Paul described himself as one 'serving the Lord', the Greek being 'slaving' for the Lord, just as a bond-slave would do the bidding of his master. But we must consider Paul's whole phrase – 'serving the Lord with all humility of mind'. The apostle's slaving and humility stand as an example and challenge to us all.

Paul was now an old man according to the wear and tear of those days, but he never slackened or stopped to waste time in excessive nostalgia. He never retired or settled back, but fulfilled his commission from the Lord to his last hour. It is his humility in particular that we wish to learn from here.

'Humility of mind' – what a term! We do not always see this on the evangelical scene today. We see people revelling in what they call authority and power and gifts, endlessly devising new methods of worship and church organisation. There is an abundance of self-confidence and self-reliance. But the motto of Paul is 'all humility of mind'.

We can understand Paul having *physical* humility because he was old, and could well have envied the energy and strength of younger workers. He was also a sick man and tells us so. So we can well imagine that he would have humility when it came to his physical limits. But Paul had '*all* humility', including humility of mind: intellectual humility.

From the reasoning deployed in his letters, we believe that Paul was a genius. It is true that his letters were inspired, reflecting divine genius rather than that of the human penman, but inspired Scripture wonderfully accommodates itself to the natural style of the writer, and so we have the impression that Paul was himself a great intellectual. Yet he possessed tremendous intellectual humility. If we read through *Romans* with an eye on the marginal references, we see the reasoning is rich with incorporated Old Testament supporting texts, both direct and oblique quotations. We see that Paul's normal practice was to go by the Book of God. He was not carried away by his powerful intellect but constantly proved his teaching from prior Scripture.

Paul's deep humility is also seen in his total dependence upon the Holy Spirit of God for spiritual power, unlike some today who behave as though power is their own innate and natural gift, available to be exercised at will. The apostle, by contrast, acknowledges that he is held in contempt and criticised for his failure to exhibit a powerful presence. He never showed off, but looked to God for spiritual enabling. Evidently he was not one of those aggressive or over-loud preachers, whose sermons are a protracted harangue, and who march up and down their platforms as though theatrical impact will secure the blessing. On the contrary, he was derided for the *relative* gentleness of his preaching.

Nor was Paul one of those people who demand blessings from God in prayer, claiming this and claiming that. Although we have great promises encouraging us to pray, we should, like the apostle, come before God with reverence and humility, as needy supplicants. All the apostle's recorded prayers are so humble. They are the prayers of one who asks and pleads, but never demands or claims.

The apostle's humility is specially seen in the modest facilities requested from his supporters, for they were so moderate. No one was ever so prepared to work with inadequate provision as Paul was. He never stopped to protest, 'Look here, as an apostle I have a right to this or that.' Even when people let him down and failed to help him, he carried on as one in the service of the Lord and submitted to him. That is humility in holiness.

We may also note the small gatherings of people the apostle was ready to serve. He never said, 'You should know that I have founded many very large churches, and have great responsibilities, and will only speak if you can assemble a thousand people.' On the contrary, at Ephesus he went from house to house, driven by his concern for souls.

Consider also Paul's humility in the acceptance of trials, as recorded in *Acts 20.22-24:–*

> 'And now, behold, I go bound in the spirit unto Jerusalem, not knowing the things that shall befall me there: save that the Holy Ghost witnesseth in every city, saying that bonds and afflictions abide me. But none of these things move me, neither count I my life dear unto myself, so that I might finish my course with joy, and the ministry, which I have received of the Lord Jesus.'

If only we could be as the apostle was in humility of mind and in the humility that accepts trials and needs, but pride so easily gets in the way. Pride is a terrible thing. It has so many forms; so many identities.

For example, there is inflexible or impenitent pride found in the person who cannot accept that he or she is wrong, and cannot apologise. People who once repented before the Lord for the saving of the soul, may, as Christians, become too self-important to regret and repent. They may lose any continuing sense of their inadequacy before the Lord. The world promotes self-confidence as the vital quality for success in life, but we turn to Scripture and see that this is the very last thing we need. Rather we need a realistic sense of our inadequacies. Let us hate self-confidence, self-reliance and self-importance. There is much repenting to do when pride breaks into the house of the soul.

Then there is a form of pride which looks for notice, for praise, for reputation, or for superiority and power and special office. Does this creep into us? It is a form of pride that does not speak its name as it enters, but comes silently. Vigilance and self-examination must be on duty to recognise and repudiate it. Related to this is the pride that wants expensive and unique things, or things that are different from what most Christians have, because possessing these things is like having a chain of office round your neck which declares: 'I am special; I am better; I am superior.' It is a terrible fall to be drawn into self-advertising, covetous pride.

Then there is the form of pride which dislikes rules and hates to be governed. It must always have its own way, saying, 'My judgement is best and I will do what I want to do.' It can come to Christians. It may have been a person's way of life before conversion, and the devil will attempt to revive it, stirring up proud self-government, arrogant individualism, or distaste for any kind of humble compliance.

When we are saved we are given humility by the Lord, this being one of the sure evidences of salvation. Pride is replaced by precious, beautiful humility, a spirit of dependence upon God, a desire to learn, and a readiness to be corrected. But what so often happens to that humility? How is it lost?

Sometimes humility is lost because we have abilities which go to our head. We dare not dwell on our abilities. We must not think too much about them, or let them elevate us above others. Remember that the gifts which matter to God are spread evenly throughout the church, and one person only possesses a small share of them. Other believers have different gifts, and we need each other, and a multiplicity of people are needed for the service of each church. God is fair in these matters, and distributes gifts to all. No believer should let the devil lie to him, telling him that he is special, and more important than others.

Here is some advice about how to deal with gifts when they go to our head. First, give some time every day, or frequently, to consider your weaknesses and your mistakes. It always humbles us to consider the other side of the coin. And then challenge yourself by reflecting not on your gifts, but on your usefulness. Think of what you have done with your gifts, and how much more you should have done with them, and should be doing even now. Think of the years in which you received far more than you ever gave in service to the Lord, and you will be humbled by indebtedness and even shame. You will see that the stewardship of your gifts has been altogether inadequate, and feel you deserve to have them taken away. It is by self-challenging reflection that we keep ourselves in hand, and hold on to our conversion humility. Remember that we are useless without God's blessing, and God hates pride. So what is the good of our gifts if the Lord finds us unacceptable?

Why was the apostle Paul so blessed, no matter what difficulties he passed through? Because he aspired to – 'all humility of mind'. He jealously preserved humility. We have known of people in the ministry who were immensely gifted and able, but who were never greatly blessed, because they allowed humility to slip away.

Sometimes, as though to teach and humble us, God turns matters on their head and chooses a person with no apparent abilities, and uses that person mightily. This does not seem to be his normal way of working but sometimes he does this, perhaps to warn those who are more gifted not to be proud. And so he makes fools of the more gifted. In the annals of Christian service we have famous examples of greatly used people who possessed no obvious gift, and we think, 'How did *they* ever have such success in their work and ministry?' Was it God warning the gifted ones that he does not bless if giftedness puffs up?

Sometimes we can be proud because we *lack* an ability, and we become envious of others, refusing to acknowledge God's distribution of gifts, and campaigning to climb above those we envy. This is what happened to Satan. This is very profound, and I can only put it in a sentence or two – but Satan became so intensely jealous of God that he refused to believe God was distinctively God. It seems that Satan began to think that God was like him, a mighty angel with whom he could compete. And so Satan took a course of action which, with his great intelligence, he would never have taken if he had continued to realise that God was God. He began to fight against God and to thwart and destroy his work, in order to be higher than God.

This is what Scripture tells us in *Isaiah 14.12-17*, the analysis of the source of Satan's horrific crime – the root of pride. Could this be the case with us, that we begin to despise people whom we secretly envy, and boost our pride by denigrating them in our mind? Our pride acts in bitterness and in competing self-elevation. Only repentance and the recovery of humility will lead us to the discovery of God's intended service for us.

If you have been given success, do not become proud and praise yourself. Recognise instead how much you owe to colleagues, fellow workers, praying believers, and most of all to God, who gives the increase. Fear pride, dear friends; it will devour your love, your mind and your years.

Some Christians become very proud of what they know. The antidote to this is to reflect on how much we do not know. Some people are even proud of the length of time they have been saved, finding superiority in this. To cure this, think about what you have done with that time, and how you will account for it. This is very humbling, and leads to deep gratitude to God for grace, which disperses the odour of pride. Satan can bring you to derive pride from holding office, or from possessions, and even from possessing a good physical build.

Let us come to the apostle's words in *Acts 20.19*, where he speaks of 'serving the Lord'. What a concept is encompassed here! As we noted, the word 'serving' strictly means 'bond-slaving', for Paul is a bond-slave of Jesus Christ. This tells us more about humility, providing both signs of humility and steps toward it.

A bond-slave is committed to the service of his master. He looks out for his every need, is receptive to his every command, and goes wherever he is sent. Humility, therefore, as we have seen in Paul, is ready to work by the Book of God. Humility keeps its eye on the Master, to obey and please him. Even preachers sometimes seem to have their eye on people rather than their Lord. They ask, 'What will attract the most people, and what will please their tastes?' Some even ask, 'What will give me a good reputation or make me well known?' The apostle looked only to Christ for instructions on methods or for approval. He never adjusted or compromised his teaching or his approach to please carnal tastes.

A bond-slave of Christ constantly reviews his conduct through humble self-examination every day, asking himself, 'What have I done? Have I offended my Lord? What are my sins of omission? Could my work be better done?' Pride seldom reviews, except in the scantiest manner, but humility often does.

A bond-slave of an emperor was always conscious of his privileges, and so are we in serving no less a Lord than the Saviour and Judge of the world. 'Why was it,' we ask, 'that the Lord worked in my unbelieving, sinful, proud heart to bring me to himself? I would never have sought or come to him of myself.' Humility remembers this often, together with the ongoing patience and mercy of the Lord.

The Newton-Cowper Museum at Olney has the framed text that hung on John Newton's study wall bearing the words, 'Remember that you were a slave in the land of Egypt.' He never forgot what God had brought him from, and this spurred him forward in dedication.

A bond-slave is accountable, and so Christian humility keeps in view the coming day when we will return our commission to the Lord who called us, to receive the undeserved eternal reward. When we find ourselves in harsh circumstances, tempted perhaps to anger, resentment or self-pity, we maintain our composure by saying in our heart, 'I am a bond-slave of the Lord, accountable to him for my reaction to everything, for my words and my manner, and I will not disappoint him or let him down.' This is humility.

A bond-slave cannot have luxuries, and humility willingly forfeits them as dangerous. Every unnecessary luxury is seen as a pride-promoting missile to the soul, and avoided. Humility is not unduly concerned about appearances. It is concerned to be smart, tidy, neat and clean for the glory of the Master, but humility does not strain to stand out as special, and to be noticed. Humility does not mix comfortably with self-promoting, self-advertising people. It does not find it enjoyable to be with those who brag and boast, and it knows how easily the bragging virus is caught.

Just as the lifelong bond-slave learned to have the interests of his master in mind all the time, so Christian humility has the cause of Christ in constant view. Occasionally we see this go wrong, even with ministers. One hears of a dispute in a church leading to the minister being hurt and offended, but his reaction is to do and say things which bring the cause into disrepute and harm the work. He is thinking of himself rather than the cause. Humility thinks of Christ and the honour of his work, not of its own vindication and comfort.

In fact, like the bond-slave of old, humility always thinks of others before itself. It is an outgoing, sympathetic virtue. Look again at the apostle's humility, and how he was able to say, 'Remember, that by the space of three years I ceased not to warn every one night and day with tears' *(Acts 20.31)*. What were these tears? They were certainly not tears of self-concern, but tears for the lost, and for the safety of God's flock. They showed the apostle's great concern that false teaching might come in and hurt the people of God. They were tears of pastoral concern when believers quarrelled, longing that they might be reconciled and restored. Humility is an outgoing, sensitive, sympathetic virtue, and if we become supportive, outgoing people, we promote humility in ourselves. The humble person wants to know how other people are faring, and goes out of his way to help.

The dedicated bond-slave both triumphed and suffered with his master, and so does Christian humility. It readily absorbs trials and troubles for Christ. Paul had so many trials. We read of some of these in the *Acts of the Apostles*, but he suffered far more than the record narrates in detail. Just look at *Acts 20.19*, where he speaks of 'temptations, which befell me by the lying in wait of the Jews'. We have some record of that, but when he puts it in the plural, we realise that unrecorded ambushes and traps were common, even continuous for him. However, he never said to himself, 'I should not be subjected to this; I should not have to put up with this; I am an apostle; I am aging and sick; this is not fair.' Humility meant that he took everything that came upon him for the sake of the ministry of Jesus Christ, and out of love and gratitude to him.

Humility, as reflected in the dedicated bond-slave, is diligent, *Acts 20.20* providing the details: 'I kept back nothing that was profitable unto you, but have shewed you, and have taught you publickly, and from house to house.' The apostle aimed at thoroughness, preaching to promote conversions, sanctification, and to furnish minds with the doctrines of the faith. He preached also to draw believers into Christian service, and to bring about their separation from the world. He preached the glorious things of Christ in all their fulness, covering everything, because humility is diligent. It is pride that preaches only the themes that are most appreciated and gain most applause.

Humility, like love, does not cling to its own interests, or even its own life. Paul was able to say, 'Neither count I my life dear unto myself, so that I might finish my course with joy' *(Acts 20.24)*. Humility is prepared to do the lowliest things: 'Yea, ye yourselves know, that these hands have ministered unto my necessities' *(Acts 20.34)*.

Humility watches for other people, whereas pride looks at number one. Humility does not covet; pride does. Remember *Acts 20.33*: 'I have coveted no man's silver, or gold, or apparel.' Humility is constantly dependent upon the Lord in prayer, and the humble Christian still commits every act of witness, every journey even, to the Lord, in prayers that ascend often throughout every day. They imprisoned Paul, derided him, counted him as nothing, and called him a madman. He was often cold and hungry, sick and exhausted, arrested and flogged, but God mightily used him, because humility is a magnet to blessing.

Pride is horrible, always starting in the mind. It goes before your every fall. It loses you true friends, surrounding you with proud people like yourself. Pride looks absurd and ugly to others. You may not recognise it in the mirror, but it is obvious to most of those around you. Somehow it stamps its signature on your stance, sometimes the very tilt of your head, the look in your eyes, and even the tone of your voice. People can tell you are proud, and strangely, even if they are proud themselves, they will despise you for it.

Pride clouds your judgement, robbing you of the perspective that makes good decisions. Pride rejects counsel, and trusts only its own conclusions. Pride is like the king in the *Book of Proverbs*, who surrounded himself with inadequate officers, and appointed fools as secretary of state and chief members of his cabinet, because he felt threatened having gifted people around him. Great is the foolishness of pride! Most people regard the proud as insincere. Accordingly, if obvious pride gets into a preacher he becomes disabled as an instrument of God. Misguided believers may admire him, but the unconverted will never trust him, thinking that he is all about himself.

Pride brews in the mind and in day-dreams. It soon infects all a person's thoughts and hopes, and if not fought early, can only be purged by a humbling fall or a sharp affliction. The Saviour said – 'For whosoever exalteth himself shall be abased; and he that humbleth himself shall be exalted' *(Luke 14.11)*. Surely this refers not only to final judgement, but to how the Lord, in mercy, deals even now to sanctify and bless his people.

Pride can lead to great laziness in witness and effort for the Lord, because the proud Christian overestimates the little he does. A minister of meagre accomplishment is probably deluded by pride to think that his small measure of effort is far greater than it really is.

In *Colossians 3.12* Paul declares: 'Put on therefore, as the elect of God, holy and beloved, bowels of mercies, kindness, *humbleness of mind*, meekness, longsuffering.' We must put on the garment of humility because we belong to God and represent him. How dare we flaunt ourselves and our imagined capabilities when we are commanded to 'be clothed with humility'! *(1 Peter 5.5.)*

We think of dear Paul, the suffering apostle, possessor of a heart burdened for lost souls, for the wellbeing of Christians, and most of all for the glory of his divine Master. We think of dear Paul, never aloof, never high and mighty, never too important for individuals or for lowly tasks. We think of dear Paul, never too sick or too old to be at full stretch as a bond-slave of Christ.

If Paul were alive today, we cannot imagine him being happy with flattering introductions at meetings, or idolising biographies. If we saw him in informal conversation with others keen to quiz him about himself, we would see *him* more interested in *them*, and in the things of the Lord. Perhaps only later would his interviewers appreciate how little they had gleaned from him, aside from his testimony of salvation and of Christ's goodness.

Let us do all we possibly can to root out personal pride, hating its every manifestation and rejecting every self-parading thought. If only it could be true of us, that we served the Lord 'with all humility of mind', how blessed we would be. Let this be our burning desire, because this is the gateway to greater personal depth and to instrumentality in the service of Christ.

12
A Life of Commitment
Seen in the Companions of Paul

OWARDS THE END of Paul's letter to the *Colossians*, written during his first imprisonment in Rome, he names seven men who assisted him at that time, men whose lives provide a definition of the spiritual life, and who continue to challenge and encourage us today. These were not the only fellow workers of Paul, for such significant pastors as Timothy and Titus are not referred to, but the 'Roman seven' have much to teach us, and in this chapter we shall assign to each one a different term to capture his distinctive attribute.

The first two to be named were travelling as bearers of the letter, Tychicus being the senior of them. Paul writes: 'All my state shall Tychicus declare unto you' *(Colossians 4.7)*. What distinguishing term can we give to this native of Ephesus, a long-time travelling companion with the apostle, who engaged in preaching, evangelism and many other duties besides? The most fitting, surely, is – *a servant.*

Tychicus had accompanied Paul as a representative of the Gentile churches when he took a great offering of relief to Jerusalem, going at least as far as Miletus with him. He was a courier for the letter to the *Ephesians*, and possibly carried *2 Corinthians* (accompanied by Titus). He was sent by Paul to Crete to minister alongside Titus, and also to Ephesus, probably to succeed Timothy. Tychicus was one of that early band of preachers who had risked their lives with Paul on his third missionary journey, and now he has been sent by him to Colosse carrying out the captive apostle's instructions.

Just look at the way Tychicus is described by Paul. He is (verse 7) 'a beloved brother', or one for whom Paul had very great affection. His character, lifestyle and love for Christ, drew out the strong affection of Paul. He also manifested a tremendous concern for Paul's work and health, being sensitive to his needs and meeting them as far as he could. To be someone described as a 'beloved brother' indicated a person of unselfish friendship and kindness, and it would appear from his record that nothing was too much for Tychicus. A servant spirit was the keynote of his life.

The apostle goes on to call him 'a faithful minister', because he cared for people. He was a preacher, certainly, but also a personal encourager and exhorter, exercising a great ministry of comfort and challenge. He had believers on his heart. Being 'faithful' also means that he was loyal to the Word, the ideal man to send to Colosse at a time when heretics were knocking at the door. He taught the Truth accurately and plainly, as one utterly bound to his high commission.

Then, as if these terms of commendation were not enough, Paul calls Tychicus a 'fellowservant in the Lord', a term rich with meaning. First, it describes him as a colleague; a team member. Tychicus, for all his strengths and capacities, was not an individualist running after his own reputation and glory. He was happy to assist the apostle and to work unobtrusively with others. He gave himself to the ministry as a diligent servant, or slave (in the Greek). A slave was owned by his master, and served his demands and comforts every hour of the day. This was the spirit of Tychicus as a servant of Christ. He would do anything that was required of him. Paul does not speak of him as a *personal* servant, but as a 'fellowservant *in the Lord*'. He would do anything for the sake of the ministry.

Tychicus will visit Colosse, says Paul, to 'know your estate', or circumstances and to 'comfort your hearts', that is, to encourage you. He will relate to your trials, share your opportunities, and do all he can to help. He will, of course, preach about Christ, lifting him up, teaching wonderful things, and encouraging you in the mission. Inevitably, he will speak of eternal glory. If your circumstances are hard, he will point your minds to the great, forthcoming, everlasting home. There was no better person for such a task than Tychicus, transparently at the disposal of the Lord, faithful to the Word, and faithful to believers. But his characteristics should be true of all of us, for this is the purpose of God's work in our hearts. Are we servants, fully at Christ's disposal, or do we run off after earthly interests? Tychicus, one of the close companions of Paul, is a pattern of unselfish love for Christ which should be the great goal of all our lives. Of course, it must be said that Paul would have naturally attracted to his band of close fellow workers people like himself, who were inspired by his life. If those of us who are ministers were more like Paul, then we would naturally gather likeminded fellow workers in our churches.

The next name to be mentioned is that of – 'Onesimus, a faithful and beloved brother, who is one of you.' Most readers will know about Onesimus, whose distinctive description must be *a trophy of grace*. A slave of Philemon, a wealthy man of Colosse converted through the preaching of Paul, Onesimus had stolen money and absconded to Rome. In due course he had somehow come in touch with Christians, and also Paul, and had found the Lord and been totally changed. Now he would be returned to Philemon and to the church at Colosse, no longer a thief and a runaway, but a servant of God. He was now a 'faithful and beloved brother', a mature believer, and a solid character who could be trusted entirely.

Are we trophies of grace? Have we really been changed? There are some people who say they have come to the Lord, but you could not really call them trophies of grace because they are not much different from how they were before. They do not seem to have a new spirit and a new heart, being entirely for the Lord and his worship and work. They are still feathering their nests in this world and getting their pleasures from earthly things. Onesimus could be sent back as a totally transformed young man, and that is what we long for in every convert. Have we truly repented of sin, sought Christ, trusted in his work on Calvary, and sincerely yielded our lives to him? Only if this is so will we be seen to be trophies of grace, with new motives and desires in life. May all readers be of the spiritual lineage of Onesimus – a trophy of grace!

Paul's third named companion is to remain in Rome, but sends his greetings: 'Aristarchus . . . saluteth you' (the word in the Greek means embraces you). He sends his fondest greetings. Aristarchus was a Macedonian from Thessalonica, and we must 'label' him as *sacrificial.* He seems to be included as the first of three Jewish helpers named. Once violently seized along with Paul (and Gaius) at Ephesus, he travelled with the apostle during the third missionary journey, and joined with him as a prisoner on 'the perilous voyage', ending in shipwreck. Aristarchus is a very notable companion of Paul. Here, he is called 'my fellowprisoner', which is both interesting and slightly confusing. He was arrested with Paul at Ephesus but that arrest did not last. Then he would have been treated as a prisoner no doubt (though not personally under arrest) on the perilous voyage. But Paul clearly means that he was a prisoner with him in Rome, and this is the point of confusion.

In the letter to *Philemon,* Epaphras is called a fellow prisoner, and Aristarchus is not. Here in *Colossians,* Aristarchus is named as a fellow prisoner and Epaphras is not. As *Colossians* and *Philemon* went out at the same time, the mystery deepens. The most probable solution is that Aristarchus and Epaphras alternated in tours of duty as voluntary fellow prisoners. In turn, they were willing to be bound like Paul in his room and be treated in exactly the same way. To stay with Paul in the hired house of his first Roman imprisonment did not allow complete freedom, because the companion could possibly have overpowered the guarding soldier and released the prisoner. To share the apostle's ministry of prayer and writing, for the sake of security, you would wear the same shackles and be treated as a prisoner of imperial Rome. Aristarchus, it appears, was one of those who was prepared to share Paul's sufferings.

The word translated 'prisoner' means a prisoner of war. Paul seems to be reminding us that he and Aristarchus were not in prison as criminals, but as captives in the world's war against Christ and the Gospel. A prisoner of war possesses a special honour in the eyes of his own nation, and Aristarchus, with Paul, may wear this title of distinction as a contender in the great battle for souls. He deserves the epithet – *sacrificial*.

Is there anything of Aristarchus in us? Do we say, 'My career is for Christ, not for me, and if I cannot rise in the world without forfeiting my service for him, I won't attempt to do it'? Certainly some believers are enabled by the Lord to get to the top *and* still serve him, the Lord opening up great opportunities of witness to them. But that is for the Lord to bring about. The rule for us is to be willing to accept a modest station in life, if necessary, to be chiefly for Christ.

Another well-known helper of Paul at this time was 'Marcus, sister's son to Barnabas', better known to us as John Mark (verse 10). What descriptive word may be assigned to John Mark? Undoubtedly that of *conqueror*. Approximately 12 to 14 years previously he had been given the great privilege of serving with Paul and Barnabas to travel, preach, and commence churches. However, in Pamphylia he deserted that missionary journey and went back to his home in Jerusalem. Why did he go? Many think he was scared in Pamphylia, being somewhat soft and unreliable. He recoiled from the threat of persecution and ill treatment. Although possessing the physical strength and energy of youth, he had not yet developed courage and persistence. His desertion was so serious that Paul would not have him back on his next missionary journey, giving great offence to Barnabas, so that Barnabas took Mark and went his own way.

In time, however, Mark conquered his weaknesses to become a leading servant of Christ, no doubt owing much to Paul's firm stand. After a dozen or more years we see his remarkable transformation. He applied himself, overcoming his lack of persistence. We see him now as an overcomer; a conqueror. He has obviously long repented of early failure and laid his weaknesses and his vulnerabilities before the Lord, who has given him character and strength to persevere. From that time he has gone forward, being instrumental in the writing of the Gospel that bears his name, which is really the Gospel of Peter, for whom he acted as scribe.

Surely we must ask: what about us? Does the earlier John Mark describe us? Do we make five-minute commitments to the Lord – undertakings that quickly die out? Do we flit from one activity to another beginning with enthusiasm, but proving unstable and unreliable? Do we have a record of numerous unkept promises to God? The self-conquering example of Mark tells us we can master our tendencies by the power of Christ. If you are a young person, moved by God to serve him with zeal, but you find yourself easily distracted and diverted, don't incur a catastrophe like Mark before you see the need to appeal to the Lord to strengthen and settle you. Stretch for greater maturity and steadfastness, and the Spirit will enable you to conquer and master yourself, so that you become consistent and reliable. It is a great encouragement to us to see Mark in the list of Paul's beloved helpers. We may all become conquerors for the service of Christ.

Another of Paul's helpers was 'Jesus *[Joshua]*, which is called Justus', who like Mark and Aristarchus was a Jew. Says Paul – 'These only are my fellowworkers unto the kingdom of God, which have been a comfort unto me.' This does not mean that these three were his only fellow workers, but that they were the only Jews among his fellow evangelists. We say fellow evangelists, because that is what the phrase 'unto the kingdom of God' indicates. They were fellow builders of the kingdom by the winning of souls. How interesting this is – that in a predominantly Gentile church there were these three conspicuous Jewish evangelists. The description fits all three, but as we know so little about Joshua Justus, not being mentioned anywhere else in the New Testament, we shall give him the epithet of *evangelist*. He is a fellow labourer unto or for the kingdom of God, bringing in the harvest of souls.

It is moving to hear Paul say that the three Jews had been a comfort, or a great encouragement, to him. We may say: 'Dear Paul, you are detained in chains, suffering great discomfort through painful ailments, and cut off from your widespread ministry, and one matter that cheers you particularly is to hear of the work of evangelists.' If only we would all be so spiritually minded, and so in tune with the heart of Christ! Here is a challenge for all of us. When we were first saved we witnessed a great deal. Do we still? We took every opportunity to pray for those to whom we spoke, and we were eager to join in other outreach activities also. Are we still? Would Paul be able to say of us, 'He is a fellowworker unto the kingdom of God, and has been a comfort [encouragement] unto me'?

After Justus the better-known name of Epaphras appears – 'Epaphras, who is one of you [a Colossian], a servant of Christ' (verse 12). What was distinctive about Epaphras? There is something that was probably true of the others also, but it particularly distinguished this brother – he was an *interceder*. Paul says he was 'always labouring fervently for you in prayers'.

Epaphras had probably been converted through Paul's ministry in Ephesus, following which he returned to Colosse and evangelised the city. Not only that city, but he apparently founded churches in Laodicea and Hierapolis too. Now he was willing to share Paul's room, being treated as a prisoner like Aristarchus. So he prayed alongside Paul. The apostle provides us with detail about the contents of the prayers of Epaphras, who laboured fervently for the Colossians, and others, that they would – 'stand perfect and complete in all the will of God'. 'Labouring fervently' is very strong in the original, the English word 'agonising' coming directly from the Greek term. Epaphras feels for the people, clearly praying for individuals and their situations, that they would progress in sanctification, knowledge and service for Christ, for all these are 'the will of God'. This also includes their preservation in purity (that they will not surrender to the threatening Colossian heresy) and that glory may be brought to Christ through the salvation of souls.

The prayers of Epaphras were not fitful or listless, nor just occasional and half-hearted, they were wrestling pleadings for the people. He asked that they would become mature and complete in the will of God, which means – God's will as expressed in his Word. In other words, he prayed that they would have a clear grasp of doctrine. He prayed for them, no doubt by name, for he knew them, and he asks that they would keep their spiritual duties day by day, and never be turned aside. That was the agenda for the prayers of Epaphras. Is it so with us?

Paul makes a kind of oath to attest the quality of the praying of Epaphras, saying – 'I bear him record . . .' He prayed as he did for three churches, constantly. If only we would be interceders of this quality there would possibly be many more churches like those three congregations throughout our land. Epaphras saluted them, and we salute him – the *interceder*!

The seventh companion to be named is Luke, and so much could be said of this remarkable man, but we shall use an Old Testament term and call him the apostle Paul's *armour bearer*, because that is what he was. So often he was there, treating the apostle's very serious health problem. We don't know exactly what Paul's chief illness was, but we know it was extremely painful, unsightly, and a handicap to him. However, Luke, the beloved physician, was often present. He was also a preacher.

A Gentile from Antioch of Syria, he was almost certainly a bachelor, and some very early references to him in tradition suggest he was also an able artist. There is an interesting theory, but it cannot be substantiated, that Luke went to university with Saul of Tarsus in that city, and some say that Apollos was also there, but not necessarily at the same time. Paul and Luke were close friends and it is possible that their friendship had roots in a similar place of education. Rather daringly, some say he was not only a doctor, but had also been a ship's doctor, or physician to a fleet. Certainly *Acts 27* demonstrates a remarkable command of correct nautical terms and maritime information.

Tradition says that Luke lived a very long life, but he still speaks today through the *Gospel of Luke* and the *Acts of the Apostles*, and the record shows that he was always ready to preach, serve, look after the apostle and, of course, to be an inspired penman of holy Scripture. Nothing can be said too highly of Luke. Although obviously a clever man and well-educated (as we see in his use of Greek), he was pledged to serve the apostolic mission in every necessary way. As 'armour bearer' to Paul he was pre-eminently a team person, and this is the challenge his life presents to us. We are all in a team as members of a church. Ideally, every capacity and ability is pledged to the Lord's service, with no one trying to stand head and shoulders above anyone else for self-notice. You can see how this was true of all the companions of Paul, but you see it particularly well in the long service of Luke.

A sadder note is struck in the case of the next named companion (verse 14), because we have to sorrow at the defection of Demas. What about Demas, Paul? Can't you say something special about him? But Paul attaches no sure commendation to this man. In fairness, he is called a fellow soldier elsewhere, but from this passage you begin to wonder whether Paul senses that Demas is not fully stable, and could suffer a fall, for this is what happened. Between five and seven years later Paul writes to Timothy – 'Demas hath forsaken me, having loved this present world, and is departed unto Thessalonica' *(2 Timothy 4.10)*.

We have not counted Demas among the seven who serve as examples to us, and the distinctive term we ascribe to him is – Demas the *unstable*. Why did Demas forsake his calling? Was he a false convert? There is no mention of this, and the discernment of Paul would surely have discovered this long before his desertion. Earlier he had been a worthy companion, carrying out good work. He undoubtedly loved Christ, but there was something deficient in his spiritual walk, and the world clawed him back by its attractions.

He was probably a very able man who realised he could earn much money and possess a beautiful house in wonderful surroundings by taking up once again the goals and opportunities of Thessalonian commerce. It could happen to any of us if we underestimate the power and the hostility of Satan, who watches continuously for opportunities to turn us back to the world. If we begin to indulge covetous desires, personal conceits, or dubious entertainments, Satan will stir our minds to desire these things increasingly, and eventually turn us away from our first love.

Demas was snatched out of service by the enemy of souls by the strategy of placing worldly luxury and acclaim in his heart. If a true believer he would surely have been restored in time by merciful divine discipline, but he forfeited his privileged work. If we find ourselves thinking too much about worldly things, over-loving earthly possessions or activities, or aspiring to self-satisfaction, we must be cautioned by Demas, the companion of Paul. Even the godly may swiftly fall. Let us cast ourselves upon the Lord asking for protection, and re-commit ourselves entirely to him. May the case of Demas, the *unstable*, warn our hearts.

Having named seven worthy companions, plus Demas, Paul has a greeting and a word for two people in the churches of Colosse and

Laodicea. One is Nymphas, about whom we know nothing, apart from the fact that a congregation somewhere met in his house. The other is Archippus (called a fellow soldier in *Philemon*). The message for him borders on the blunt: 'And say to Archippus, Take heed to the ministry which thou hast received in the Lord, that thou fulfil it.'

What had he done, or what was he not doing that he should have been doing? It is likely that Archippus served as pastor in the church meeting in the house of Philemon *(Philemon 2)*. Some say he was Philemon's son, set aside for the ministry of the Word. What was the matter with him? Was he lacklustre? Possibly it was something like this. He was clearly an earnest young man who loved the Lord, and truly wanted to serve him, but Paul seems to say, 'Why don't you get on with it?' Perhaps he is not preaching the Gospel as he should be, tirelessly bringing in the lost and teaching the people. Something is distracting him, so we will call him Archippus, the *distracted*.

You see it today, even in the ministry. I know of a most able pastor who wrote a number of edifying books, and very long ones, while his church fell to pieces. He became distracted, and stopped evangelising. His writing totally engaged his emotional energies. His chosen field may have been good, but it took his time and attention from his primary ministry. I can think of one or two ministers who have been chairmen of numerous missionary societies and other boards, but as they travelled here and there to chair this and that important meeting, their churches lay at death's door, with no increase. These brethren have been sound, but sound asleep. Perhaps they needed the apostle to say to them, 'Take heed to the ministry which thou hast received in the Lord, that thou fulfil it.'

Our motto should be – First things first. There is much to do; there are souls to win; there are people to build up, and we should be doing those things. I am not speaking about pastors who are distracted by sinful things, and worldly things, but some who have been distracted by secondary activities. Something else, however worthwhile, has interested them and taken their attention from their most important calling. Only recently a missionary was telling me that there is a tendency in some lands for new missionaries to be planting Bible colleges before they have developed a single credible church, and before they have opened a Sunday School. Paul really says to Archippus – 'First things first, and get on with it.'

It is not only ministers who may be distracted. Years ago I knew a young man who was conspicuously poor at being involved in any Christian service, but he was busy writing a 500-page book telling other Christians how they should live. The apostle's word to him would certainly have been – 'Take heed to your share of the labour commitment to your local church.'

Are we distracted by other things? We hear that some professing Christians spend weeks and weeks planning their holiday travel, rather than serving the Lord, while others devote all their spare time to home or hobby or sport. Perhaps some reader who sincerely loves the Lord errs in the wavering of his direction, and needs this same word – 'Take heed to the ministry which thou hast received in the Lord, that thou fulfil it.' We think that this word would have transformed Archippus the distracted, and galvanised him for years to come.

Most of the companions of Paul were marvellously committed people and we can learn so much from them. Think of Tychicus with his true *servant* spirit. O, to be like him – all for Christ and entirely at his disposal. Then think of Onesimus, a *trophy of grace*; a completely changed young man. May our own transformation at conversion last, and our graces grow and flourish. Think of Aristarchus – so *sacrificial*. Today, except in persecuted regions, we are not called upon to become voluntary prisoners. All our sacrifices are so much easier to make, and we should make them gladly. Think of Mark, the *conqueror*, who overcame his weaknesses by the power of the Lord. There is hope for us, for we can all make progress for Christ.

Think of Justus the *evangelist* who so encouraged Paul. What do we do, by way of individual or corporate witness, for Christ? Think of Epaphras the *interceder*. Would British churches be declining if we were more like him? And what of Luke, Paul's *armour bearer*, who, for all his outstanding education and abilities, willingly took a supportive role, and received the privilege of human authorship of *Luke* and *Acts*? How we need his humility and vision for teamwork!

Only Demas the *unstable* disappoints, his experience calling us to self-examination. And lastly Archippus the *distracted*, an earnest and good brother, no doubt, but one who needed a kindly jolt to order his priorities aright. Paul's epistles are all so *pastoral* that even the greetings are a blessing to us, if we heed them. And the insights we receive about his co-workers are a challenge and inspiration to all who, down the centuries of the Gospel age, seek to maintain active personal spiritual lives.

Sermons of Dr Masters, audio or video,
may be downloaded or viewed free of charge on the
website of the Metropolitan Tabernacle:
www.metropolitantabernacle.org

The Lord's Pattern for Prayer
118 pages, paperback, ISBN 978 1 870855 36 5

Subtitled – 'Studying the lessons and spiritual encouragements in the most famous of all prayers.' This volume is almost a manual on prayer, providing a real spur to the devotional life. The Lord's own plan and agenda for prayer – carefully amplified – takes us into the presence of the Father, to prove the privileges and power of God's promises to those who pray.

Chapters cover each petition in the Lord's Prayer. Here, too, are sections on remedies for problems in prayer, how to intercede for others, the reasons why God keeps us waiting for answers, and the nature of the prayer of faith.

God's Rules for Holiness
Unlocking the Ten Commandments
139 pages, paperback, ISBN 978 1 870855 37 2

Taken at face value the Ten Commandments are binding on all people, and will guard the way to Heaven, so that evil will never spoil its glory and purity. But the Commandments are far greater than their surface meaning, as this book shows.

They challenge us as Christians on a still wider range of sinful deeds and attitudes. They provide positive virtues as goals. And they give immense help for staying close to the Lord in our walk and worship.

The Commandments are vital for godly living and for greater blessing, but we need to enter into the panoramic view they provide for the standards and goals for redeemed people.

Faith, Doubts, Trials and Assurance
139 pages, paperback, ISBN 978 1 870855 50 1

Ongoing faith is essential for answered prayer, effective service, spiritual stability and real communion with God. In this book many questions are answered about faith, such as – How may we assess the state of our faith? How can faith be strengthened? What are the most dangerous doubts? How should difficult doubts be handled? What is the biblical attitude to trials? How can we tell if troubles are intended to chastise or to refine? What can be done to obtain assurance? What are the sources of assurance? Can a believer commit the unpardonable sin? Exactly how is the Lord's presence felt?

Dr Masters provides answers, with much pastoral advice, drawing on Scripture throughout.

For a full listing of Wakeman titles please see www.wakemantrust.org